Understanding 8–9-Year-Olds

Understanding Your Child Series

The Tavistock Clinic has an international reputation as a centre of excellence for training, clinical mental health work, research and scholarship. Written by professionals working in the Child and Family and the Adolescent Departments, the guides in this series present balanced and sensitive advice that will help adults to become, or to feel that they are, "good enough" parents. Each book concentrates on a key transition in a child's life from birth to adolescence, looking especially at how parents' emotions and experiences interact with those of their children. The titles in the Understanding Your Child series are essential reading for new and experienced parents, relatives, friends and carers, as well as for the multi-agency professionals who are working to support children and their families.

other titles in the series

Understanding Your Baby
Sophie Boswell
ISBN 978 1 84310 242 7

Understanding Your One-Year-Old
Sarah Gustavus Jones
ISBN 978 1 84310 241 0

Understanding Your Two-Year-Old
Lisa Miller
ISBN 978 1 84310 288 5

Understanding Your Three-Year-Old
Louise Emanuel
ISBN 978 1 84310 243 4

Understanding 4–5-Year-Olds
Lesley Maroni
ISBN 978 1 84310 534 3

Understanding 6–7-Year-Olds
Corinne Aves
ISBN 978 1 84310 467 4

Understanding 10–11-Year-Olds
Rebecca Bergese
ISBN 978 1 84310 674 6

Understanding 12–14-Year-Olds
Margot Waddell
ISBN 978 1 84310 367 7

Understanding Your Young Child with Special Needs
Pamela Bartram
ISBN 978 1 84310 533 6

Understanding
8–9-Year-Olds

Biddy Youell

155.42
YOUELL
2008

Jessica Kingsley Publishers
London and Philadelphia

Extracts from *Suddenly...99 Short Stories for the Millennium* on pp.44–45 are reprinted by permission of ChildLine/NSPCC.

First published in 2008
by Jessica Kingsley Publishers
116 Pentonville Road
London N1 9JB, UK
and
400 Market Street, Suite 400
Philadelphia, PA 19106, USA

www.jkp.com

Library of Congress Cataloging in Publication Data
Youell, Biddy.
  Understanding 8-9-year-olds / Biddy Youell.
    p. cm.
  ISBN 978-1-84310-673-9 (pb : alk. paper) 1. Child psychology. 2. Child development. I.
Title. II. Title: Understanding eight-nine year olds.
  BF721.Y833 2008
  155.42'4--dc22
                        2008002558

British Library Cataloguing in Publication Data
A CIP catalogue record for this book is available from the British Library

ISBN 978 1 84310 673 9

Printed and bound in the United States by
Thomson-Shore, 7300 Joy Road, Dexter, MI 48130

Contents

Acknowledgements

I would like to express my gratitude to all the children and families whose stories are featured in this book. I am particularly grateful to ChildLine for permission to reprint stories from their Millennium collection.

Foreword

The Tavistock Clinic has an international reputation as a centre of excellence for training, clinical mental health work, research and scholarship. Established in 1920, its history is one of groundbreaking work. The original aim of the Clinic was to offer treatment which could be used as the basis of research into the social prevention and treatment of mental health problems, and to teach these emerging skills to other professionals. Later work turned towards the treatment of trauma, the understanding of conscious and unconscious processes in groups, as well as important and influential work in developmental psychology. Work in perinatal bereavement led to a new understanding within the medical profession of the experience of stillbirth, and of the development of new forms of support for mourning parents and families. The development in the 1950s and 1960s of a systemic model of psychotherapy, focusing on the interaction between children and parents and within families, has grown into the substantial body of theoretical knowledge and therapeutic techniques used in the Tavistock's training and research in family therapy.

The Understanding Your Child series has an important place in the history of the Tavistock Clinic. It has been issued in a completely new form three times: in the 1960s, the 1990s, and in 2004. Each time the authors, drawing on their clinical background and specialist training, have set out to reflect on the extraordinary story of "ordinary development" as it was observed and experienced at the time. Society changes, of course, and so has this series, as it attempts to make sense of everyday accounts of the ways in which a developing child interacts with his or her parents, carers and the wider world. But within this changing scene there has been something constant, and it is best described as a continuing enthusiasm for a view of development which recognizes the importance of the strong feelings and emotions experienced at each stage of development.

In focusing on 8–9-year-olds, this book describes the "latent" stage when children gradually move away from reliance on their family and become more concerned with the outside world. Children of this age start to develop a greater sense of right and wrong, often becoming concerned with questions of justice in usually clear-cut good and evil situations, and they tend to become zealous about environmental issues and making a difference to the world. They also commonly like to explore the worlds of mystery and fantasy through books and films. Biddy Youell skillfully describes aspects of the eight- to nine-year-old's development, and offers approachable and clear advice for parents and the professionals who work with them.

Jonathan Bradley
Child Psychotherapist
General Editor of the Understanding Your Child Series

Introduction

What is distinctive about the eighth and ninth years of life? What can parents and teachers expect of children in this age group? How do eight-year-olds differ from their ten-year-old siblings, or indeed from their six-year-old brothers and sisters?

Looking at any one age group cannot, of course, be an exact science. A group of eight- or nine-year-olds will vary enormously in their physical, emotional and psychological maturity. In every individual child an enormous amount of change and development takes place between "just eight" and "nearly ten". This book will inevitably offer a picture made up of generalizations; a picture against which to measure the individual eight- and nine-year-olds we know, whether as parents, relatives, friends or professionals. As well as an outline of what might be thought of as "ordinary" features of this stage, each chapter will look at some of the complicating factors and possible variations in children's experience and development.

This is the period of childhood which we call "latency", a period in which children have a rest from some of the turbulence and passion of the early years and turn their attention to the outside world. The gradual moving away from total reliance on the family continues as children develop their relationships outside the home and face a range of new tasks and challenges. School has been a feature of life for about three years but in some areas it changes at this point into something a little more formal: the transfer from infant school to junior school at age seven in the UK is one of several significant times of transition in a child's school career.

Questions of identity move beyond the confines of the family. The child is no longer simply the child of his or her parents but an individual who feels defined in a more complicated way. Children will describe themselves not only by name, but also by school, by year group, by neighbourhood, by favourite soccer team and possibly by friendship group.

When all is going well, and there are firm foundations to build on from the child's earlier experience, these "latency" years are about the mastery of new skills and the accumulation of knowledge. Children are finding out about the real world, at the same time as enjoying forays into the world of fantasy, magic and mystery. They are developing a sense of right and wrong and may become very preoccupied with questions of justice. The world is often seen as consisting of "goodies" and "baddies" and there is a strong preference for stories in which good triumphs over evil and there is a happy ending. Causes such as the protection of endangered species are very appealing to children in this developmental stage and they may become zealous about environmental issues such as energy conservation or recycling. They need to believe they can make a difference and may be overwhelmed by some of the harsher realities of life.

Children of this age tend to revel in making collections, whether it be of various kinds of stickers, "Top Trumps" cards or "Bratz Kids" accessories. These collections also provide the focus for some element of rivalry and competition, as well as an arena for the assessment of relative value and the development of bargaining skills. Children respond enthusiastically to being awarded badges or stickers and thrive on praise and recognition.

Eight- and nine-year-old children vary enormously in their physical development. Some are beginning to stretch out and look as if they are just waiting to move into adolescence. Others are still round-faced and somehow toddlerish. By the age of nine, there may be some girls who have begun to menstruate, although this sign of physical maturity is unlikely to be matched by emotional or psychological development. For the most part, this is an age group in which boys and girls opt for friendships with their own gender and are intolerant of the other.

The ensuing chapters will look at aspects of the eight- to nine-year-old child's development, with examples drawn from real experiences in a variety of family, community and school settings. All names and identifying details have been changed.

1

The Family

Parents

The family is central to the child's life whatever his or her age, but in this middle period of childhood, we see the beginnings of a move away from such close dependency. Eight-year-old children are developing their own social world, albeit on a very small scale, and are less preoccupied than hitherto with their parents' lives, less possessive of one or other parent and less jealous of the adult couple. In early childhood there is usually a passionate attachment to parents. Young children have strong emotional ties to both their parents, but often go through a phase of being particularly preoccupied with one or other of them, usually the parent of the opposite gender. In *Understanding Your Three-Year-Old*, Louise Emanuel (2005) gives a vivid account of the Oedipal feelings which are a normal part of childhood experience. She describes a little girl who dresses up to greet Daddy each evening and a little boy who does his best to occupy the front seat of the car and dispatch his father to the back. Both are examples of children who are looking ahead to a phase of life in which they will be adults with the potential for adult relationships. In early childhood, these imaginings are focused on the adults they know but by the time a child reaches eight, there is a loosening of these Oedipal ties. Boys no longer imagine that they will grow up and marry their mothers and girls come to accept that they cannot have sole possession of their fathers. The result is a turning towards their own gender, with boys identifying with their fathers and other boys, and girls with their mothers and other girls.

Parents are sometimes puzzled by the way their eight-year-old no longer seeks to sit himself between them, or inveigle himself into a central place in their bed on a Sunday morning. Suddenly, he is moving his face away from his mother's goodbye kiss at the school gate and when he finds his parents exchanging a kiss and a cuddle in the kitchen, he is no longer consumed with jealousy, but leaves swiftly, muttering "Yuck" under his breath. His interest in sexual matters is more likely to be focused on what he picks up in the playground, where sexy talk is rehearsed alongside jokes and rhymes about lavatories and farting. The aim is to be as risky, shocking and "filthy" as possible and the content of the talk is entirely divorced from ideas of love and family.

Of course, the fact of parental sexuality may force itself into the notice of the latency child in a variety of circumstances. The break-up of a parental couple presents the latency child with a number of new challenges, as does the arrival of a new partner for a lone parent. A more ordinary challenge to the child's wish not to notice the parents' sexuality is a pregnancy and the arrival of a new baby in the family.

> This was exactly what happened to disturb the world of eight-year-old Sam. He had been in the comfortable position of being both the "baby" of the family and the playmate of his older brother, William. He had been able to follow his brother and his friends into the social world of the park, returning home for a reassuring cuddle when things moved too quickly for him. He could choose whether to keep pace with his brother or stay home with his mother. When she became pregnant and a baby sister arrived, his world was shaken. He struggled to be as grown-up and accommodating as William but found it almost impossible to control his emotions. He was angry with his father (unconsciously aware of his father's part in producing the baby) and rejected the extra attention on offer from that source. He competed for his mother's attention, particularly when she was most in demand from the baby. He would insist on her helping with his homework or arrive in the room with a grazed knee just at the point when she was preparing to breastfeed her crying daughter. William also avoided the sight of his mother feeding Sophie but his was a more 10-year-old response. "Oh gross! I never did that did I?"
>
> The boys' school contacted the parents to express their concern. Sam was moody and difficult in class. He was rude to teachers and seemed to dissolve into tears at the drop of a hat. At home, Sam tried to show interest in the baby but he could not be consistent and would offer a favourite cuddly toy one minute and grab it back with a surreptitious pinch the next. The children's mother found Sam's behaviour distressing. She was angry with him but felt guilty about his suffering.

Should she have held back from having the third baby she and her husband had both wanted?

Things were difficult for a few months but quite suddenly the picture changed. One evening, Sam met his father at the door, declaring excitedly, "Sophie had some soup today. The same soup as the rest of us!" Sam's father had been greeted with news of Sophie's achievements before but this event seemed to have particular significance. What it marked was the near completion of weaning. Sam had not been able to tolerate the intimacy between his mother and Sophie in the breastfeeding relationship. As soon as this phase was over and Sophie became more interesting, an individual who was both mobile and verbal, Sam was able to "forgive" his parents and slip into the role of Sophie's adored older brother.

Parents and their latency children

Parents vary enormously in how they relate to their eight- and nine-year-old children. Some couples take the opportunity to revitalize their own social lives and develop their own interests, leaving the children to develop theirs. If they are frank, many adults find the latency world of their eight- and nine-year-old children much less interesting than the turbulent emotional world of the earlier years. In other families, this is the period when the adult and child worlds come together, with parents and children sharing interests and activities. This may be particularly evident between fathers and sons, and mothers and daughters, though not exclusively so. Some families seem to move around as an inseparable unit, with the adults devoting themselves to the demands of the children's lives. Many parents now include the children in what might previously have been thought of as their own special events, such as anniversary celebrations. This may suit adults whose own interests are congruent with those of their children and it is certainly true that there is greater acceptance these days of grown-up men and women retaining an interest in some "latency" activities, particularly perhaps those with a technological component. Boys and their fathers may compete in computer skills, with fathers anxious not to be left behind by their digitally literate sons. It has always been the case that eight- and nine-year-old boys have joined their fathers in activities such as fishing, while others have become junior members of their father's sports club. The gender divide holds true for many mothers and daughters, with girls often accompanying their mothers on shopping trips and developing a keen interest in clothes and hairstyles.

There is, of course, a very real sense in which this is a stereotypical and therefore an incomplete picture. There are many families in which boys and girls divide up differently and parents encourage non-gender-specific activities. There are also many communities in which children follow very clear culturally specific pathways in terms of their developing interests and skills.

Siblings

A child's position in the family is always of great significance. An eight- or nine-year-old who is the oldest child may take on a number of "parenting" tasks, while an only child of that age may still occupy the position of "baby" in the family. What about the eight- or nine-year-old who is in the middle of a group of siblings? At some stages in life, being in the middle has its disadvantages, but for children in middle latency, there are distinct advantages. It enables them to fade a little into the background in order to pursue some of the developmental tasks which characterize this phase of life. They can leave some of the turbulence and passionate struggles to the toddler and the young adolescent whilst they occupy the hinterland, busy with the accumulation of knowledge and skills and the gradual development of social connections outside the home.

Where there are a number of children, the quality of the relationships between the siblings will be a key factor in the general well-being of the family. Older children help younger children to understand what is in store for them at school. They introduce them to the ways of group play in the park, the neighbour's back garden or wherever children gather locally. Young children long to be as big, as skilful, as popular as their older siblings. Eight- and nine-year-olds will look up to a teenage sibling while seeing it as their responsibility to protect the younger ones. An influential ten-year-old brother can be a protective factor for his sister in the year group below. All she has to do is mention her brother and the bullies will back off. Even when brothers and sisters disparage each other in various ways at home, they are likely to leap to each other's defence at school. One nine-year-old hated having to walk to school with his younger sister and would do whatever he could to detach himself enough for it to be unclear as to whether they were walking together. He would cringe with embarrassment if she and her friends hung around when he was playing football or was just being "cool" with his mates. However, if she fell in the playground or was upset about some perceived unfairness, he was quick to intervene.

Children sometimes have to support each other more comprehensively in the face of pressures at home or at school. In extreme circumstances, where parents are preoccupied with their own worries, siblings need to be able to turn to each other for comfort. Where a parent or parents are largely absent from the home because of work commitments or because they cannot cope with the demands of parenthood, children of latency age can be extraordinarily resourceful. Some sibling groups form functioning family units where the practical tasks are shared out and emotional support is freely given. Children with parents who have physical disabilities or who suffer from mental illness may succeed in keeping the household together, whilst also attending school. Of course, there are many examples of families where the burden on the children is way beyond what is reasonable. Where there is serious neglect or active abuse, children of eight or nine may take full responsibility for younger siblings and will be likely to do their best to keep the reality of their situation hidden from their teachers and their peers.

Jay, aged nine years, came to school every day but he was nearly always late and often looked as if he had had no sleep. His clothes were grubby and there was sometimes a strong smell of stale perspiration. He ate his school lunch with relish. His teacher often enquired after his mother and younger siblings, but Jay said very little in response. When it was suggested he could come in early for breakfast club he reacted angrily, saying there was plenty of breakfast at home. When his teacher asked why he had not brought back a signed slip to say he could go on a museum visit, he said he did not want to go. After a particularly difficult week in which Jay fell asleep twice, lost his temper and then burst into tears when asked to read out loud, the headteacher was informed and he arranged for the education social worker to make a home visit. The state of the home was shocking and Jay's mother was extremely defensive. A referral to Social Services resulted in a full assessment of the family's needs and Jay eventually talked about the violence between his mother and stepfather and the way in which he looked after his four-year-old sister. As well as making sure that she had enough to eat, he slept on the floor near her bed to protect her.

Sibling rivalry

All sibling groups have times when they fall out, but brothers and sisters who are constantly "at war" are a source of anxiety, frustration and exhaustion for parents. Much may depend on the way they themselves managed and continue to manage their feelings about being in their particular position in their family of origin. We tend to think of sibling rivalry as being between an older child and new baby (as with Sam in the example earlier). However, there are many younger children who seem not to be able to bear the fact that they were *not* the first. This may lead them to strive to emulate their older sibling and match his or her achievements, but it may equally result in a child who constantly feels inadequate or hard done by.

> After a number of years as an only child, eight-year-old Ayesha was thrilled to have a baby sister, Jess. Everyone was surprised by how readily she accepted the newcomer and how helpful she was to her mother in the early weeks and months. She loved it when her mother brought the baby to meet her at the school gate and she could show off the fact that she had a sister. It came as a great shock to the family that when Jess became mobile, her main aim seemed to be to approach Ayesha to scratch or thump her. At first this was amusing, but Ayesha became tired of it and felt very hurt by this unexpected hostility. As Jess grew older, the hoped-for improvement in the relationship never came. Their mother would do her best to show Jess how mean she was being but Jess would not relent. She was a friendly and popular child in her nursery and infant school but her hostility towards her sister continued. She would scream if Ayesha touched her toys or took up a position next to their mother on the sofa. Ayesha eventually gave up her attempts to be close to her sister and began to use her superior vocabulary to belittle Jess's achievements.
>
> When Jess was eight and Ayesha was 16, the situation suddenly changed. Ayesha was developing a full social life outside the home and Jess was more relaxed as a result of having more of her mother's undivided attention. The arguments just seemed to melt away and Jess even expressed some admiration of her fashionable teenage sister. For the first time, their parents were able to imagine their daughters enjoying a mutually supportive relationship in adult life.

Most sibling rivalry is manageable within ordinary family life and does not take as long to resolve as the hostility between Ayesha and Jess seemed to take. However, chronic jealousy between siblings is one of the pressures which can create discord between parents. It may be that a mother and father have very different ideas as to how to manage the arguments or they may become split as to which child they see as the aggressor and which the victim.

Mr and Mrs Davis were worn out by the endless fights between nine-year-old Chenice and seven-and-a-half-year-old Jason. They had tried everything they could think of to keep the peace. Privileges such as sitting in the front of the car were allocated in strict rotation. Birthday and Christmas presents had to have exactly the same monetary value and both children were provided with a television in their bedroom in an attempt to avoid the arguments over television programmes or possession of the remote control. Mealtimes were a nightmare with accusation and counter-accusation flying across the table. Jason mocked his sister's food faddiness and Chenice complained that his table manners were making her feel sick. Chenice provoked her brother by going into his room uninvited and he retaliated by emptying her school bag over the floor just as it was time to leave the house. Both children felt they were entirely justified in taking their revenge when they had been wronged.

Mr and Mrs Davis became more and more desperate as they tried to ensure that the children were treated fairly; it was like living in a courtroom. One morning, things unexpectedly reached crisis point. Mrs Davis told Chenice that as she had been late getting ready for school, Jason could sit in the front of the car. She did not realize that handing a forfeited privilege to the "innocent" child served only to fuel the hatred and resentment. Chenice sat grumpily in the back, kicking Jason's chair as he hummed in an irritating, self-satisfied way. She asked him to stop, then shouted at him and then swore. She burst into tears of rage and he called her a cry baby and said that he would tell everyone at school. She kicked him again and he wriggled out of his seat-belt to reach over the back of his chair to hit her. Mrs Davis put her arm across to restrain Jason and as she did so, swerved into the oncoming traffic. Fortunately, there was no collision but Mrs Davis was shaken and that evening, told her husband they had to do something.

They visited their family doctor, who referred them on to the local Child and Adolescent Mental Health Service. In the safety of the clinic setting, they were able to acknowledge that they both secretly "blamed" the other for the predicament they found themselves in. They also had differing views as to which of the children was more to blame. Mr Davis believed that his daughter would be well behaved if it were not for Jason's provocation. Mrs Davis was more inclined to see Jason as the injured party. After all, he was younger; Chenice should be able to control herself.

Further exploration of their differing viewpoints revealed factors from their own childhood experiences which were impacting on their current behaviour. Chenice and Jason listened intently as their parents spoke about their own siblings and about the way their parents had dealt with conflict in the respective homes. After this, the children were able to acknowledge that they wished they did not fight so much and really wanted both parents to be able to intervene and stop them. A new agreement was made that they would try to get on better and that if one got in trouble, the other would not expect to benefit from it. Mr Davis agreed to spend time on Saturdays doing something with Jason while his wife spent time with Chenice.

Grandparents

Grandparents can be hugely important to children of this age. If they play an active part in the life of the family, grandparents make a significant contribution to the developing sense of identity in the latency child. Eight- or nine-year-old children are able to grasp the idea that these are their parents' parents and in getting to know them, children can begin to understand something of why their parents are as they are. The two sets of grandparents represent family history and children of nine are usually interested to piece together simple information about past generations on both sides of the family.

In the early part of the twenty-first century grandparents may represent a different age and generation in a way which parents might not. It sometimes seems that the generation gap has narrowed with parents hanging on to aspects of their own youth culture.

> This was the case for Melissa. Her mother and father were up to the minute in terms of technological know-how, they each owned a portable media player and they wore jeans and trainers at weekends. Melissa was proud of her "trendy" parents but she loved spending time with her paternal grandparents, whom she saw as very different. Her grandfather referred to her digital audio player as her "transistor thing" and repeatedly asked her to help him with managing the sophisticated video recorder and hard disk drive player which he had bought but could not operate. She liked it that her grandmother worried about her wrapping up warm on cold days. They showed more interest in her school work than did her parents, who rather took it for granted that she was doing well. They loved to be invited to school concerts and she was very proud to be seen with this distinguished looking couple.

The only area of discomfort for her was being forced to recognize that the relationship between her mother and these much loved grandparents was not such a good one. She could not understand what the problem was between them. It pained her to listen to her mother complaining about always having to include them in family events and then to listen to her grandmother's barely disguised criticisms of her mother's cooking or cleaning. Grandmother could not come to terms with her daughter-in-law going out to work and made no attempt to hide her views. She was always willing to step in to babysit, but invariably took the opportunity to comment that this meant Melissa's mother was going out again and then to observe to Melissa that there was a pile of ironing waiting to be done. Melissa would try to stop her doing it, knowing that her mother would be angry and then her father would become defensive.

Melissa much preferred to go to her grandparents' house, where she spent hours looking through family photos. Meals here were more formal affairs than at home but she liked Grandma's cooking and so did not mind fitting in. She would occasionally get back home and take her parents to task for their relatively lax table manners. This did nothing to improve the relationship between Melissa's mother and her grandmother!

Things were very different at her other grandparents' home. She went there less often because it was much further away, but she loved the shabby, overcrowded feel of the house and made firm friends with the resident pets – a dog and three cats. These animals had been acquired soon after her two uncles and her mother had left home and the grandparents were devoted to them. Melissa loved to curl up on the sofa with the dog while her grandmother settled into her chair with the cats draped around her. There, Melissa was allowed even more freedom than at home and she and her grandparents would often share pizza and ice cream, eaten unashamedly in front of the television.

Both sets of grandparents provided Melissa with opportunities to stay away from her home and her parents for short periods of time. She enjoyed going to both houses, although she often commented that they were so different. Her paternal grandparents insisted on a set routine, cocoa and a bedtime story at an agreed time with lights out half an hour later. Her mother's parents did not seem concerned about bedtimes and she would sometimes fall asleep in the living room or take herself off to bed when she was too tired to stay up any longer.

Melissa's experience is not untypical. Families where there is complete harmony across two or more generations are relatively rare. Melissa could see the tensions between her mother and grandmother and between the two sets of grandparents, but for the most part, everyone behaved well at family gatherings. Melissa could see that their values were not fundamentally different and that her parents had found a way to manage areas of difference between them.

Many families do not manage things so well and many latency-aged children find themselves playing a part in complicated family dynamics. They may be pulled in one direction or another, or may be under instruction not to behave in a particular way or not to tell a grandparent something. In more extreme circumstances they may be caught up in family feuds or never have the opportunity to get to know grandparents who are estranged from their children. Some grandparents are intolerant of young children and find eight- and nine-year-olds too noisy, too precocious, too opinionated. Having grandchildren is often a welcome second chance to play a part in bringing up a child. It can, however, be an unwelcome reminder of earlier failures and may stir up intolerance, hostility and resentment. Indeed, some grandparents do not manage to control their envy of their children and grandchildren's lives and are grumpy and critical as a result.

Many families in the early twenty-first century depend on grandparents to provide a crucial childcare function, so that mothers can go to work. This may be a matter of choice, where there is agreement that a grandmother is the best carer available for the children, or it may be a matter of necessity. Childcare services are expensive and when parents are working in low-paid jobs, it may be that the grandparents step in to support the household economy. By the time children reach eight years of age, the involvement is likely to be reduced to after school time, with grandparents picking children up from school and looking after them until parents finish work. This may include deeply significant parts of the daily routine, such as the evening meal, homework and bedtime rituals. Children develop very close and important relationships with one or both grandparents in this way and are then massively affected by their grandparents becoming elderly or unwell.

> Grandma Sadie collected Sally Ann from school three days a week. She loved to watch her granddaughter emerge from the school door, surrounded by her friends. She had vivid memories of standing in the same spot, waiting for Sally Ann's mother some 35 years earlier. She never ceased to feel moved when Sally Ann spotted her, and said her

goodbyes before coming over and giving her a big hug. They would chat about the day as they walked to Grandma's house, where the rule was that they would look together at Sally Ann's homework before turning on the television. Grandma Sadie made lovely teas – all Sally Ann's favourites. When her father came to pick her up, he always found them sitting companionably on the sofa watching television and he felt slightly cruel when he then wanted Sally Ann to hurry and get her coat and school bag.

One cold winter day, Sally Ann came out of school and Grandma Sadie was not there. She waited a few minutes before going back in to the secretary's office, where she waited for another hour while the secretary tried to make contact with her grandmother and then with her father at work. It was six o'clock before her father arrived, looking pale and shaken. In the car, he told Sally Ann that her grandma had fallen outside her house and was in hospital with a broken hip. She had suffered a very minor stroke. The hospital had called Sally Ann's mother at work. Sally Ann was very upset and wanted to go straight to the hospital but her father said that six o'clock was too late; they could visit her the next day. Sally Ann was stricken and when she got home, upset her mother by being difficult about supper. She wanted Grandma's cooking. Didn't they understand? Friday was always sausage and chips! Sally Ann remained in a grumpy mood through that evening and the next day. Her parents thought she would be better when she had seen Grandma but when the time came, she said she did not want to go. She insisted she was too busy with homework to spare the time. Her mother got very cross and accused her of being selfish and ungrateful.

Sally Ann did go and see Grandma and was a little bit reassured. She took her some grapes and magazines and seemed relieved to see that she was not so very different. However, the ensuing months saw Sally Ann and Grandma Sadie having to renegotiate the terms of their relationship. It was a long time before Grandma could walk back and forth to the school and she needed much more help than before with carrying shopping, cooking and other household chores. Sally Ann had to get used to being her grandmother's helper and she did not always manage it with a good grace.

The relationship was strong enough to emerge from this phase in good shape. There would have been changes anyway. Sally Ann would inevitably have reached a stage of being less appreciative of her grandma's attentions. What was so painful was the way it had happened so unexpectedly, just when they were both enjoying their comfortable routine.

In the best of circumstances grandparents offer a safety net to latency-aged children in all kinds of ways. They can sometimes step in to negotiate on behalf of the child, or can provide back-up for parents who are struggling to manage difficult situations with their eight- or nine-year-old children. Children who feel safe with grandparents have somewhere to go if things at home are problematic; somebody to talk to who cares about both them and their parents, but who brings a different perspective to bear on things. Grandparents who live nearby become part of the fabric of the child's life. Those who live far away, or in contrasting circumstances, may represent variety, difference and a sense of adventure.

Extended family

Much of what has been said about grandparents can apply to the role of uncles, aunts and cousins. Each individual relative has a part to play in the child's life and therefore in the child's developing sense of self. Uncles and aunts often play an important part in the life of an eight- or nine-year-old, offering an alternative role model to the mother or father, but representing a "safe" adult who is connected in a significant way. Cousins, rather like siblings, offer all kinds of opportunities for experimenting with relationships. Some cousins will be admired, others disparaged. Some will stir up protective feelings in the eight- or nine-year-old child and if there are cousins of a similar age, there may be the opportunity to try out some competitive or rivalrous feelings in a safe context.

Family breakdown

Parental discord or marital breakdown can be a serious obstacle to the eight-year-old who is trying to distance himself from his earlier preoccupation with intense feelings for his parent or parents. Mothers and fathers whose relationship is breaking down are hard pressed to protect their children from the emotional fallout, even when they try their best to do so. Many separating couples agree to succeed in convincing their offspring that the break-up is really not anybody's fault and that the children remain of central importance to both parents. All too often, however, these good intentions become eroded by the reality of divorce proceedings. Even where marriages end through mutual consent, powerful feelings of hurt, suspicion and jealousy often translate into bitter wrangling over financial settlements and arrangements for the non-resident parent's contact with the children. Where there is a new partner, these conflicts may be even more acute and children will inevitably witness the suffering of the "abandoned" parent.

Some couples do, of course, manage an amicable break-up, with arrangements for contact with children being agreed and adhered to without too much difficulty. The non-resident parent may be included in significant family events and may be a welcome visitor in the family home. This is obviously beneficial to all concerned but there is one small drawback. It can leave latency-aged children confused as to why their parents could not continue to live together and may lead them to harbour unrealistic hopes of reconciliation. The following story is probably a typical one.

> Daniel had always known that his parents were not as happy together as he thought they should be. He knew that his mother suffered with something called "depression" and that his father was not very sympathetic about it. He could see that his mother did not look forward to his father coming home at the end of the day. Indeed, he had noticed that she was less gloomy when he was working away from home for a few days. On these occasions, she made special suppers for him and his sisters and they would all curl up on the sofa watching programmes his father did not like. He had loved his mum with a passion when he was very young and he still carried a lock of her hair in a little box in his pocket. He was very sad that he could not make her happy. He also loved and admired his father and treasured the times when he fetched him from school in his fast car or came to watch soccer practice.
>
> Daniel was nine when his father announced that he was leaving home. His initial response was one of shock, quickly followed by an intense feeling of responsibility. He would now be the man of the house and his mother and younger sisters would need him to be strong. He gave his mother a hug and reassured her that they would be OK. He told his father that he would look after the family. His father promised that he would stay closely in touch and that there would be no money worries.
>
> For the first few weeks, Daniel chose to believe that the separation was a temporary one. His parents seemed to be getting on fine and surely they would realize how much they missed each other? He concentrated on trying to make sure that he and his sisters made no

demands on either parent, giving them plenty of time to talk and realize their mistake. He did not know at this point that his father had a new partner. When this news broke, the nightmare began, particularly for Daniel, who found that his mother could not contain her distress and began to tell him all kinds of things he did not want to know. He was desperate to hang on to the version he had been told. He did not want to know that his father had set up home with another woman and that the affair had been going on for two years. He did not want to hear his mother talking about his father to his friend's parents or to his grandparents.

He began to feel angry with his mother and to blame her for his father's departure. She should have made him stay. He did not articulate this in a way which might have led to a proper talk with his mother but instead, he began to moan about lack of pocket money, embarrassment about being seen in her grotty old car and so on. She was hurt and so the cycle of accusation and counter-accusation got going. She suggested he was just like his father and he shouted back that he wanted to be like his father. He told his sisters that they were the problem; the family had been happy until they came along.

For the first six months, Daniel kept up his angry tirade against his mother. He desperately wanted to see his father and suspected that his mother's fury was making it impossible for him to come to the house. In his mind, he split the parental couple into the innocent victim (father) and guilty party (mother). This was a split based entirely on the nature of his own understanding of his own suffering at the time. The split was reversed over the next six months when he began to realize that his father was not being prevented from visiting but was actively choosing not to. He was let down on a number of occasions. He began to feel more supportive of his mother again, although he would not let her criticize his father in his presence. He felt the loss of a male role model in the home, but he had a male teacher and was able to make the most of the time spent with his uncle, his mother's younger brother.

New families

A different kind of intrusion on the "latency" state of mind occurs when a parent becomes involved in a relationship with a new partner. Daniel, in the example above, was never really able to accept his father's new girlfriend. He agreed to meet her and was polite enough for a period of a few hours, but he did not want to visit their house and point blank refused to go to their wedding. He knew this hurt his father but his loyalty to his mother had by this time become entrenched and he was very scathing of his sisters, who seemed much more willing to compromise in the interests of keeping everyone happy.

The arrival of a new partner may be particularly challenging for the child who has become used to living with a single parent. Some children actively want a second parent (mother or father) for themselves or for the parent they view as lonely, unprotected or in some way incomplete. However, some children who have had sole possession of a parent over many years do not find it easy to accommodate a third person.

Here are two very different examples.

Janice's mother suddenly (from Janice's point of view) announced that she was going to go out one evening a week to a salsa class. Janice was shocked and asked "Why?" Her mother explained that she used to like dancing and that now that Janice was eight and her brother was five, she felt that it would be OK to leave them with a babysitter and begin to build up a bit of a social life for herself. Janice repeated "Why?" as if unable or unwilling to believe that she could possibly want more than to be their devoted mum. When the evening of the class came, Janice made a rather half-hearted attempt to get her mum to stay at home, complaining of a stomach ache and saying she thought she might be going to be sick. Recognizing her ploy for what it was, her mother said that she was sure she would be fine and that her grandparents would cope if she were sick. She added that she would have her mobile phone with her if there was any real crisis. Janice sighed and allowed herself to receive a goodnight kiss. She could not get to sleep but when her mum came home and peeped into Janice's room, she was generous enough to pretend that she was sleeping soundly. Tuesday evenings became a favourite with the children, who enjoyed their grandparents' company. When their mother suggested a second night out, there was a slight rise in Janice's anxiety level but she managed not to complain. Getting used to the idea of a new babysitter was much harder but she soon realized that there were compensations; she could get the babysitter to let her stay up a bit longer and could negotiate extra time watching television.

A different story unfolded in the Bailey family when Tommy's mum said she was going to go out for the evening to a neighbour's house.

Tommy immediately became hysterical and he forbade her to go. She was so taken aback that she quickly telephoned her neighbour and reassured Tommy that she would not leave him. Over the next six months, leading up to Tommy's ninth birthday, she made several attempts to go out but it always ended the same way. Tommy would become frantic and she would back down. Mrs Bailey found she could not bring herself to stand up to him. He was so distressed that she decided she would rather stay at home than watch him suffer. She told herself that he really needed her to be there. If she invited anybody in for the evening, Tommy would come downstairs to join them, refusing to go back to bed until the visitor had left. He was particularly rude to male visitors and his mother began to feel that she would never be able to make new friends or build a social life for herself. When she lost her temper one evening, Tommy took a knife from the kitchen drawer. She did not believe that he would hurt her or hurt himself, but it shook her confidence. They were church-goers and so she tried to get the vicar at the local church to talk with Tommy. When this did not work, she tried to take him to the family doctor; Tommy kicked up an enormous fuss and ran out of the building. She did not try to take him again, but she did begin attending a series of appointments herself and in her sessions with the counsellor came to understand what might be behind Tommy's behaviour.

Tommy's father had disappeared when Tommy was just ten months old. She had been shocked by his desertion of them and then very angry. She did not know where he was but heard that he had been involved in a fight on the estate. For months, she shut herself into the flat with her baby, terrified that somebody would come looking for them. She would go into the bedroom with Tommy and push furniture up against the door. She slept badly, listening out for noises through the night, and huddling close to Tommy's sleeping figure. Over time, she regained her confidence and she made peace with her parents, who had never approved of her partner. The counsellor suggested that Tommy might be suffering from a complicated cocktail of feelings. As a nine-year-old boy, who had been in sole possession of his mother for so many years, he was beset by jealous feelings in the face of her desire to make new social contacts. When these feelings were stirred up at night-time, they would become very confused with those early experiences of shock and terror, of being shut up with a tense and frightened mother. The resulting panic was overwhelming and neither of them could manage it.

This was not an easy problem to solve. Mrs Bailey realized that she had to tackle the situation by taking advice, agreeing strategies and sticking to them. She also knew that Tommy needed help to address the underlying issues: unresolved feelings of loss in relation to his father, fear of losing his mother, doubts about her feelings for him if she were to make room in her mind for anybody else. After some mother–child work, focusing on Tommy's life story and then on the immediate separation problems, Tommy was able to start individual psychotherapy sessions. He was reluctant to engage with a therapist but did eventually allow himself to be interested in the process.

Family groupings

There is now an enormous range of family groupings represented in any community. In a typical class of eight- to nine-year-olds, there will be children who live with one parent, both parents or neither parent. Of those who live with a lone parent, some will see the non-resident parent regularly; others will not know the identity of the absent parent. Some will be in the care of the local authority, living in foster families. Some may be adopted; others may be living with grandparents or aunts and uncles. Some children have a gay parent or live with gay foster carers or adopters. It is no longer acceptable, or accurate, to refer to the two-parent family as the only "normal" family constellation. The debate goes on as to what is desirable for children's healthy and secure development but the sheer variety of family constellations now accepted as "ordinary" does mean that children are not exposed to so much mindless prejudice. It is no longer so difficult for children to tell their peers that their parents have split up, that they do not see their father or that their mother has a new partner.

This is the public face of family life and it is important not to minimize the effect of these differences on the private lives and internal worlds of children. It may be relatively easy to tell your classmates that you don't remember your father and that you don't care, but the effect at a deeper level may be very much more significant.

Denise lived with her mother and three younger siblings on a run-down estate on the edge of town. Her father had left when she was six and the next child, a boy, was four. The twins were born two years later but their father did not live with the family. Denise was pleased because she did not like him much and was jealous of the attention he paid to the twins. Denise was very proud of her mother's ability to provide for the four of them and loved her home, particularly her bedroom, which had been redecorated just before her ninth birthday. Her brothers shared a room, which felt a bit unfair, but her mother said that as she would soon be ten and thinking about secondary school, she should have a bit of privacy. Her mother did not know how much time she spent in her room looking at photographs of her father and imagining what it would be like if he came back. She longed to see him, or even just to hear news of him. There had been nothing since her seventh birthday. She constructed all kinds of stories about where he was and why he did not get in touch.

Soon after her birthday, Denise decided to send a letter to her father. She did not know his address but thought that her grandparents would send it on. She knew where they lived, even though they had not wanted to see her or her brother since the twins were born. In the letter, she wrote that she missed him and wished she could see him, suggesting that she could meet him somewhere if he did not want to come to the house. She was thrilled when she got a reply. He wrote, saying that he missed her and would come to take her and her brother out the following Saturday. She was hesitant about telling her mother and very relieved when her mother seemed to take it in her stride, saying that she understood Denise's feelings.

At school, Denise told everybody that her father was taking her out at the weekend. She was in a state of high excitement by Friday and slept very little. When her father arrived, she looked at him with shining eyes and grabbed her coat, shouting at her brother to hurry up. She tried to ignore the tension between her parents as she and her brother hopped from foot to foot in anticipation. When they came back a few hours later, her mother let them in. "Well?" Denise shrugged and answered "OK". Her mother asked lots of questions but Denise clammed up.

This is a fairly typical story, with a nine-year-old having to manage her complicated feelings about an absent and neglectful parent. She has held on to her idealized memories of her early relationship with him and hopes to rekindle something by making contact as she approaches puberty. It seems that the real reunion has not lived up to her fantasy and she returns from her outing in a deflated state.

Children in care

The experience of children in foster care is even more complicated and the deep-seated sense of loss and insecurity all too often shows itself in erratic or confrontational behaviour. Children who have experienced neglect or abuse in their birth families and multiple placements in the care of the local authority have little reason to trust the adult world and very little chance of relaxing into the kind of "latency" development described in this book. Even the most experienced foster carer can be shocked by some of the challenges thrown down by a hardened, cynical nine-year-old boy or can find themselves deeply disturbed by an eight-year-old girl who seems worldly-wise beyond her years. If a child has been sexually abused, he or she may have a distorted view of adult life and will need help to understand the ordinary boundaries of relationships in a family and at school. It is sometimes difficult for parents to know whether a child with a background such as this presents any kind of risk as a friend for their son or daughter. So long as parents have confidence that their own child is sensible, all that is probably needed is a heightened degree of supervision for everybody's peace of mind and protection. Close liaison with foster carers or social workers is also important. Children whose lives have been disrupted desperately need the adults around them to hold together in a thoughtful way. They do not have experience of a parent as an ordinary reference point for making sense of the world. They do not have a parent to go to, to make ordinary requests about what they can and cannot do. The foster carer has to check everything with Social Services. Depending on the nature of the legal order, permission for outings or sleepovers may have to be sought from a birth parent. Friends' parents have to be thoroughly vetted. It is not surprising that "looked after" children can become cynical, expecting to be let down by the system. Of course, when the system works well, children can thrive in good foster homes and in school communities which are aware of the complexities of these children's lives.

Alternative role models

As has already been noted, the latency child becomes less dependent on the parent or parents and begins to look to other role models in the adult world. This has probably happened at an earlier stage in relation to the child's teacher but the array of preferred adults now extends to include the soccer coach, the piano teacher and the best friend's mother! Parents are sometimes hurt by how much their nine-year-old likes being in other children's houses. It is not always easy to remember that this is a necessary stage in what will ideally be a slow and steady separation from home and that it is possible only when children feel secure in the knowledge that they have a home to return to. Some children who face deprivation, neglect or abuse in their own home may gravitate towards the homes of their more fortunate friends and this can provide a helpful counterbalance. It can also set up complicated situations with children harbouring fantasies of being "fostered" and adults finding that they feel responsible for the needy child they have welcomed into their home. Some parents fall all too readily into the role of "rescuer" and quickly get out of their depth, needing a grandparent, teacher or possibly social worker to help them work out what they can or cannot provide for a child who is not their own.

Even in the best of circumstances, eight- and nine-year-olds are on the lookout for alternative adult role models and so are vulnerable to stepping into positions which satisfy the needs of adults. This is one of the reasons, perhaps, why this age group is so often targeted by adults whose motivations are exploitative rather than benign. "Stranger danger" is so well publicized in present-day society that children are often hypervigilant and too ready to be suspicious of a stranger's attention. It is all the more remarkable then that children do fall prey to the tactics of paedophiles. This can be understood in terms of the children's need to feel that they are of interest and value to somebody and that they can manage situations for themselves. The following example was given by a teacher in a work study seminar.

Ellen and Paula told me that they could not come to netball practice because they always visit Mr Grant on Tuesdays after school. I asked who Mr Grant was and they explained that he lives in one of the basement flats on Pembroke Street. I asked how they knew him and they said that he had stopped them on the pavement months ago and asked them if they could help him carry his dustbin up the basement steps. He gave them sweets to say thank you and now he has sweets ready for them every Tuesday. I asked tentatively whether their parents knew Mr Grant and they both shook their heads. Ellen said that they would not like him because he was a bit dirty and swore when people threw litter into his basement area. I tried to sound very calm and not to jump to conclusions and asked if they liked visiting him. They looked at each other before Paula said, "Not much", but added that they could not stop because he would be so sad. He was very lonely. I asked if they had told their parents and they shook their heads silently.

Ellen then said that she did not like the fact that he wanted to give her some money and Paula said quickly, "He's lonely, that's all."

It was clear to the teacher that she could not ignore this conversation. She did not want to over-react but felt worried about the story, particularly when it came to the mention of money being offered. On the other hand, the neighbourhood was full of lonely, elderly people and these were sensible girls who would not do anything stupid. The argument went back and forth in her mind as she made contact with the girls' parents (having told the girls that she would need to do so). She was not sure how the two sets of parents would respond. Would they see it as a risky but manageable situation or would they cry "paedophile" and ban their children from walking down that street. Would they step in and go with the girls? What was clear to the teacher was that the girls were reacting in a way which was entirely consistent with their developmental stage. They wanted to make a difference, believed they could and had only a partial awareness of the risks involved.

2

Play

Play continues to be a very important part of life for the average eight- and nine-year-old child.

> All kinds of anxieties and conflicts are worked through in play. Oedipal concerns and ideas about separation, loss and sibling rivalry (real or imaginary siblings) get acted out and rendered less frightening in the process. Children try out all kinds of identifications – playing the role of mother, father, baby, policeman, doctor, super-hero, and many more. Most children are very aware that they are playing and manage to regulate their emotional engagement with the drama. Only if the feelings become too intense or convincing do children need to extricate themselves and check back with the real world in the shape of parent or teacher. In this sense, play acts as a bridge between the conscious and unconscious realms of experience, between the external and internal worlds of the developing child. (Youell 2006, p.46)

In the latency years, there are significant changes in the way most children play. In line with their new-found enthusiasm for absolute fairness, children of eight or nine tend to gravitate towards games with clear rules. Their aggressive impulses are channelled into competitive sports and board games in which they can outwit their opponent. They do not always manage games of chance very well, feeling that it simply "isn't fair" if the roll of the dice goes against them. Competitive games of all kinds are useful training grounds for managing feelings of hope and triumph as well as of feelings of disappointment and failure.

Children of eight and nine probably still enjoy dressing up and role-play but this may begin to take the shape of plays with a prescribed plot and a rehearsed script. At this age, children tend to be more concerned about the detail of their costume; particularly girls who become engrossed in copying hairstyles, make-up and nail polish (see cover picture). They also enjoy a range of craft activities, especially those which involve shiny materials and lots of cutting and sticking. Glitter and sequins are a firm favourite of almost every eight-year-old girl. It is not by chance that children's television shows, such as the BBC's *Blue Peter*, enjoy such longevity. In line with the rest of children's programming, its presenters are now younger, trendier and more excitable than their predecessors but the basic format remains the same. The programme, and others like it, still manages to reflect the essence of the latency years, with items focusing on the natural world, good causes, individual achievements and high adventure, as well as on models and novelty items which can be made by anybody at home, with the minimum of equipment and resources.

Play and learning

By nine years of age, the distinction between play and work has been established and play in school is now seen as confined to the playground or to those precious moments of "Golden time" earned through hard work or good behaviour. Of course the dividing line is less clear in the minds of children and they often stray across the line without intending to do so, adopting a decidedly "playful" approach to a work task. This playfulness may or may not get in the way of learning. In the example which follows, it can be seen to have been a very positive element in a numeracy lesson for nine-year-olds.

> The class was asked to sit on the carpet while the teacher recapped on yesterday's lesson and explained the task for today. The children were to work in pairs, conducting their own simple survey and plotting their results on a bar graph. They were given a few ideas as to what question they might ask of their fellow classmates. The teacher suggested they could find out about each other's favourite foods, colours, lessons, pets, sports teams and so on. The buzz of excitement and competition grew as she talked, most of the children looking around and whispering loudly to claim their preferred partner. Many jumped up and began to shift chairs and grab pen pots. The teacher had to call them back to check that they knew what to do and then she had to

sort out the many small skirmishes which had erupted about who was working with whom. Predictably perhaps, most of the boys opted to ask a question about British football teams, while the girls chose to ask about favourite pets. The classroom became a hive of activity as the children drew their tally charts and began to ask each other their questions. They rushed around the room, falling over furniture and each other as if it were a race. It quickly became obvious that the boys were heavily invested in making sure that their own favourite team got the most votes. In short, they cheated, but they did so in an entirely open and often witty way. Once they knew what the teacher would say (West Ham), they either avoided asking her or asked her several times! They offered inducements to people who would say "Chelsea" or got on their knees to beg a small timid newcomer (who could speak little English) to utter "Manchester United". The girl pairings were almost as passionate about the animals, one pair cheering each time somebody voted "dog", another trying to persuade everyone to say "rabbit".

The teacher asked them to keep the noise down but decided to be flexible about time because she had rarely seen such engagement with a task. Not surprisingly, the resulting graphs were inaccurate, with absolutely no consensus among the groups as to the results. However, the lesson had been fun and the class had grasped the basic principles of tally charts and bar graphs. The teacher said she would return to the topic the next day and emphasized the need for accuracy.

It was interesting to see one boy, Reuben, who did not have a partner with whom to work. His teacher told him that he should make up a threesome but after several rejections, he gave up on this idea and worked alone. He completed his graph with speed and efficiency and showed it to the teacher, who congratulated him, held it up for the class to admire and told him he had earned some play. He made a show of cheering and punching the air but then did not seem to know what to do with himself. He went to the book corner and flopped onto a beanbag, from where he watched the rest of the class, whilst aimlessly fingering some magnetic shapes on the board behind him. He looked longingly at the groups of giggling children.

Children can be very cruel about making pairs, organizing themselves into groups of three or picking teams for a classroom game. As soon as the teacher indicates that she wants them to divide up, the atmosphere becomes charged with anxiety and competition. Children hate to be the one who is left out. Close observation of a class group will reveal that they are capable of nasty tactics to secure their place and exclude somebody else. In the example above, Reuben was rejected a number of times. One pair flapped at him silently; another told him, in a whisper, to "f*** off". A third pair pushed him away physically, shoving him in the small of his back. The last pair he approached appealed to the teacher, "Miss…we don't want him. We don't have to have him, do we?" There was obviously a history to this sequence of events. The observer later learned that Reuben was a very clever boy who tended to take over if he worked in a group.

The school playground

Playtime is a very important part of the school day. The average eight- or nine-year-old needs a break from the classroom and will probably benefit from a few minutes in the fresh air. However, a typical school playground offers something much more complicated. It is a social world in which children find out about themselves, about friends and friendships, about belonging and being left out, about their own strengths and weaknesses, and about hierarchies based on age, gender, skill or sheer physical strength. For some children, the playground is a terrifying place which they will do anything to avoid. These are the children who are always willing to do a job for their teacher in the lunch break or who look at the sky as playtime approaches, praying for rain. For others, playtime is their opportunity to excel, to lead and to impress. The playground is the place in which many children try out their social relationships, especially at this age when they are beginning to be interested in the idea of belonging to a group as well as having a special or best friend. It can, of course, be a dangerous place if there is inadequate supervision.

Eight- and nine-year-old children in the playground are usually involved in the full range of activities. The "sporty" boys might be playing soccer, sometimes managing to join in with the games of older boys, who accept them to make up the numbers or because there is one particularly talented player in the younger group. Many schools have had to stop boys from bringing balls in to school because of the way in which they become the focus for coercive bargaining or outright bullying.

There may be other traditional playground games. Particularly popular with girls of this age are games of hopscotch or skipping. However, there will also be groups of children huddled on benches or leaning on walls, exchanging news and jostling for position. Some pairs may be wandering around on the periphery, girls linking arms and turning away from anyone who tries to break into the twosome. Teachers of eight- and nine-year-olds have commented that this is a fascinating year group because the children really want to get into groups but cannot actually manage it; most are still at the stage of needing the security of knowing they have a best friend, even if the best friend changes from time to time. They cannot manage too much conflict.

Play at home

Children of this age may have certain chores and responsibilities outside school, but there is still an expectation that play in the broadest sense will be much of what the child does in the evening, at the weekend and during holidays. Play might be seen to include a whole host of options: organized sports, riding bikes or scooters, roller blades, construction toys, board games, playing with dolls or model cars, computer games and many more. Some are solitary activities; others require the participation of another, be it a parent, sibling or friend. Some require a number of participants and probably an adult to supervise or organize. For many families, most of the available "free" time is devoted to passive watching of the television and the debate rumbles on as to just how damaging this is (or isn't) for children's development. It is easy to generalize and to idealize the pre-television era when (we are told) families found their own entertainment and parents were much more likely to play with their children. We cannot be sure how much has been lost and whether the benefits of television and other technologies outweigh the disadvantages. However, it is becoming clearer that children who cannot play, those who can neither participate in games with others, nor occupy themselves in a creative way when alone, are at a distinct disadvantage when it comes to their learning and their social relationships.

Playing alone

There are children of eight or nine who never try to join in with others and never seem to seek out the interest or approval of an adult. They are sometimes mistakenly characterized as "independent" or "self-sufficient" when it may be more accurate to think of them as children who have not had the opportunity to play in the presence of a playful, attentive adult, sharing and celebrating their achievements. The lone play may be a desperate attempt to hold themselves together, to hold anxiety at bay and deal with their loneliness. If it is a very entrenched pattern, it may be that the child has created an illusion of self-sufficient omnipotence and genuinely does not want company. Observing a child in solitary play may show that he or she is engrossed in a vivid imaginative life. Very often, close observation reveals that the child who is thought to be in a world of his or her own is in a rather barren, lifeless place.

Limited play

Imitation is an important element of play but it is a cause for concern if a child's play is purely imitative. Close observation of role-play (pretend play) may reveal that some children are trying out identities and developing stories in their minds about the activity, whilst others are simply repeating sequences with no development and little enjoyment. These are the children who, for example, arrange furniture and dolls in a doll's house in an accurate way but never develop a story about the house or its occupants. These may be the children who go on to prefer copying to free drawing and who will have difficulty with creative writing.

Among the group of children whose play is largely imitative may be some who cannot manage imaginative, symbolic play because of some actual or partial failure in their capacity to differentiate between fantasy and reality. They cannot reliably tell the difference between what is real and what is pretend. Traumatized children very often suffer from this kind of confusion.

> One example of this comes from a primary school classroom where a support teacher found herself having to reassure Iqbal that the model of a volcano which the class had made together would not actually erupt. He had suddenly frozen in front of it and when she commented on this, he asked her in a strangled voice whether the lava would reach his estate. Iqbal was a child who had come to England with his parents as a result of being made homeless through flooding in Bangladesh (Youell 2006, p.44).

There are children whose traumatic lives have left them hyperaroused and hypervigilant. They may be, unconsciously, on the lookout all the time for the next assault and will react nervously to noises which pass most children by, such as aeroplanes passing overhead, a cement mixer in the street outside the school or a distant siren.

Children who have this kind of permeable boundary between reality and fantasy (between what is real and what is pretend) can be problematic playmates. They can start a game of rough and tumble in a playful way but respond to an accidental knock by becoming violent and serious about wanting to hurt the other person. Competitive games of all kinds can erupt in this same way, with the competition becoming all too real for some of the players. Vulnerable nine-year-olds can start a game of *Monopoly*, for example (whether the traditional board game or a state-of-the-art electronic version) knowing that they are playing with pretend money, but as the game progresses can become over-identified with extreme wealth and power or over-fearful of poverty and failure and the game becomes real in their minds. This is different from the ordinary grip of competitive rivalry, which can take hold of any of us to some extent and which is an important part of learning to compete and to win and lose.

Traumatized children sometimes get caught up in some re-enactment of the trauma; the activity looks like play to start with but tips over into something much more real. A vivid example of this was a child who had been beaten at home before being removed and placed in foster care, smacking a teddy in play and then becoming frantic as he beat the teddy harder and harder and smashed it against the floor. Children who have been sexually abused or exposed to inappropriate sexual behaviour sometimes confuse physical affection with sexual touching and they may be taken over by sensuality when in physical contact with another child or an adult.

In these situations, adults need to be the ones who can recognize what is happening and intervene as necessary. Particular vigilance is required when these vulnerable children are engaged in animated computer games. The debate about whether or not violent games produce violent children often misses the point. It is usually concerned with the nature of the game and does not take into account the state of mind of the player. Nine-year-old children who have a clear sense of what is real and what is imaginary, and know when they are playing and when they are not, are unlikely to be adversely affected by a level of violent excitement in a game. They may also know when they should stop playing and remind themselves of the real world in order not to become too frightened. The child without a secure internal world and a reliable sense of what is real may become overwhelmed by the game, over-excited and in danger of becoming addicted to the over-excitement. The real world may then become dull and uninviting by comparison.

Puzzles and non-fiction

There are a large number of children who do not actually confuse real and pretend but who have a marked preference for reality. These are the children who will prefer factual books to fiction and who may lean towards games such as jigsaws, number puzzles and some computer games. They like certainty and are reassured by knowing that there is a "correct" solution to a problem. They are also reassured by being able to repeat the same procedures over and over again and always to achieve the same outcome. Popular culture is not kind in its labelling of this sort of child as "nerdy" or "a bit of a geek".

This group of children usually do well in most aspects of formal education and are not usually a trouble to their teachers. They may, however, become socially isolated, avoiding contact with peers and opting, wherever possible, to work independently. If being asked to join another child or a group in a different kind of activity causes intolerable anxiety, there may be a need for further exploration of the child's overall well-being. It is usually a question of degree.

> Philip was a tall, skinny boy with pale blue eyes and a distant expression. He was brilliant at maths and loved to bury himself in a challenging calculation. Numeracy hour was his favourite part of the school day; literacy hour his least favourite. When it was time for reading he would gravitate towards books which were packed full of information – facts and figures about machines, vehicles, volcanoes and dinosaurs. His teacher tried to interest him in stories but he could not really see the point. His own compositions were always heavy on information and light on fantasy.
>
> Philip did not mind being called a "train spotter". If somebody yelled "anorak" at him in the playground, he would turn calmly and say "Yes…and so what?" He was not worried about it and neither were his parents. He got on well enough with his siblings and cousins; children in his own class did not mind working with him. His aptitude for maths was useful in small group work.

> Donald's predicament was rather different. He was also good at maths but not exceptionally so. He was completely obsessed with modes of transport, particularly trains and buses. He could quote the bus timetables for most routes in the town and spent his weekends at the junction of his street and the main road, noting down their comings and goings. Donald did not manage social relationships in the classroom or at home. He preferred to sit alone and would begin to sweat and breathe heavily if required to sit close to other children, even his sister. He was terrified of any activity which was not firmly

rooted in irrefutable fact and would deal with his anxiety by becoming loud and aggressive.

At home, Donald was content so long as he was left alone to get on with his own interests. He did not react well when expected to join the family at mealtimes or to go out with them to events in the wider community. Changes in routine, or alterations to arrangements, sent Donald into a spin. He hated family holidays above all things. All of this made life very difficult for his parents and sister. They felt that his need for a predictable life restricted them to an intolerable degree. Donald himself seemed not to care. So long as his needs were prioritized, he was indifferent to their feelings.

Donald's parents consulted his school and together they arranged for a full assessment of his abilities and needs. An educational psychologist conducted a battery of tests at school and they sought a referral to a paediatrician at their local hospital. Some months later, Donald was given a diagnosis of Asperger syndrome. They expected him to mind but he did not seem to; if anything, he seemed a little relieved to have a label to counter the insults he got at school. His parents were able to read up on the condition and joined a group for parents which offered support and advice as to how best to cope with their son's special needs. They began to be able to attend to the needs of their daughter and also to take time for themselves, individually and as a couple. At school, measures were put in place to support Donald in managing his anxiety and he was given individual help with subjects he found threatening.

3

Literature and the Eight- to Nine-Year-Old

Children in the latency years are often caught up in imaginary worlds. They have usually come to terms with the fact that Father Christmas and the tooth fairy do not actually exist but they are still very attracted to a world of make-believe. Favourite stories are likely to include those where the central characters have extraordinary powers. Many take the form of cartoons or computer-generated creatures. Animals, toys, robots and machines have minds and can speak. If human children are the subject of a story, they will probably be in groups which are faced with all kinds of challenge and adventure. Stories about ordinary lives are relatively rare and when they do feature they are often stories in which children set off into a situation without their parents. Thinking back to the popular stories of the second half of the twentieth century, we see the Famous Five and Secret Seven series of books (Enid Blyton) where groups of young children are pitted against criminal gangs, or *Swallows and Amazons* (Arthur Ransome) where a group of children take on all kind of adventures whilst sailing on their own in a small dinghy. These books are set in a world which has disappeared, if it ever really existed, and certainly one which seems incongruous in a society which is so concerned with health and safety.

More recently, we have seen the popularization of the *Chronicles of Narnia* (C.S. Lewis) *Lord of the Rings* (J.R.R. Tolkien) and other classics through television and film. The stories and characters are made accessible to children who are not yet old enough to read the original texts or who would be unlikely to have access to the books outside of the school setting. The stories, whether in books or on film, share some common themes. They are almost all concerned with the struggle between good and evil and in most cases good prevails. Terrible things can happen along the way, and most children will enjoy a measure of shock or suspense, but they are reassured when things work out for the best at the end of a story.

Opinions differ as to whether children of this age group should be actively protected from sad endings or from stories where the "baddy" triumphs over the "goody". Many contemporary children's authors have written stories which address real-life issues such as bullying, family break-down and adoption and they are immensely popular with children of this age group. They are attractive to children who recognize aspects of their own experience as well as with children who have no direct experience of the kind but who are intrigued by it. The work of Jacqueline Wilson, for example, makes some parents and teachers feel very uncomfortable but many children choose to read them and there is very little evidence that they produce undue anxiety or distress.

This raises an important issue in relation to this age group, as to any other. There is a huge discrepancy between what some children can take in their stride and others will find impossibly disturbing. Sometimes this is due in a straightforward way to the gap in emotional development between one eight-year-old and the next. In an average classroom reading session, some eight-year-old children will be looking at books where the picture tells the story, supported by very simple text. Others will be deeply engrossed in the latest gargantuan volume of the Harry Potter series by J.K. Rowling. Some-times, however, the gap in development is of a different and more serious order. There are some children who do not have a clear sense of the difference between fact and fiction and they can become very confused in the face of a powerful story, film or television programme. This issue was looked at more closely in relation to play and inhibitions in play.

Children's stories

The stories which children themselves write are usually very revealing of their interests, worries and preoccupations. The following selection is from a book published in aid of the UK charity ChildLine at the end of the year 1999. The task was to write a story about the Millennium in 99 words, starting with the word "suddenly".

Jane Anna Locke. Age 8¾

Suddenly…Mum stormed through my bedroom door. "Your room is a mess again," she shouted. "This is your last warning, Jane!" Her voice faded as she went downstairs, murmuring, "Wait till Daddy gets home." I lay on my bed, ignoring the chaos around me, and wondered how to celebrate this Millennium thing. In a flash, the solution came to me! I tidied, polished and put everything away. Mum will be pleased, I thought. After all, this is a Millennium coming soon and this is the thousandth time, according to Mum, that she's told me to clean up my room.

This story has many elements which are typical of an eight-year-old girl. First is the way that she gives her age as 8¾. The fact that she is nearly nine is clearly very important to her. She then chooses a scene from family life, but one which shows her as very slightly rebellious, almost adolescent. She sees the link between the thousand years of the Millennium and the well-known phrase "I've told you a thousand times" and builds her story around this joke.

Louise Allcock. Age 8

Suddenly I woke up. I was not in my bed but at the bottom of the garden and was only three inches tall. I was stood next to the Millennium Fairy, she told me her name was Millennia, she had come from her house to deliver presents for the new Millennium. She asked if I wanted anything and she gave me a box. On the side of the box it said the magic of the Millennium. When I opened the box lights of the Millennium magic glowed around me, my eyes opened and I was safely in my bed again.

This story is less polished than the previous one in its punctuation and in its use of humour, but it is again very typical of the age group. Louise is taken with the idea of what it would be like to be very small, to be a miniature version of oneself. There is magic in the story and a beautiful fairy who can bestow gifts, but who can also ensure that at the end of the story, the main character, Louise herself, is safely back in her own bed. Eight-year-olds are very attached to their own beds and much prefer stories to have happy endings.

Adam Ladd. Age 9

Suddenly the Millennium Bug appeared. At the Houses of Parliament it tickled the computers until they laughed their monitors off! Without their computers the MPs couldn't remember their speeches, so they went home. In Tokyo all the wires inside the computers turned into noodles. The bosses threw them out and people came with their chopsticks and ate noodles until they were full. In America the space shuttle wrote "HELLO MUM" in the sky on its way into orbit. When everybody celebrated New Year the bug was scared away by the sound of bagpipes and was never seen again.

Nine-year-old Adam has a well-developed sense of the absurd. His story differs from the two eight-year-old girls in that he does not make himself the main character. There is no "I" in this story. He demonstrates that he has knowledge of a world beyond his own home; he knows about different countries and he has an idea of the world of work – computers, MPs (Members of Parliament) and bosses. However, his preoccupations are surprisingly similar in that the story involves ideas of magic and it has a happy ending. Perhaps most interesting in this example is the way in which, in the midst of the chaos and excitement, "Hello Mum" is woven into the narrative. The nine-year-old storyteller does not stray far from home for very long.

Humour

In common with seven- to eight-year-old children, eight- to nine-year-olds love the fact that they can understand jokes, riddles and rhymes. They indulge in endless "knock, knock" and "elephant" jokes and enjoy making up their own words to well-worn songs. Here are two examples, the first told by an eight-year-old twenty years ago and the second just last year. They are different in content but similar in spirit.

> Just one Cornetto,
> Give it to me,
> Not b***** likely,
> It's 60p!

> Mary Mary quite contrary
> How does your garden grow?
> I live in a flat, you stupid prat
> So how the f*** should I know?

Both were considered slightly risqué by the children who sang them, largely because of the use of swear words. Most eight- and nine-year-olds prefer humour which is based on jokes rather than on clowning around or slapstick. They may laugh at a good custard pie routine or the up-to-date equivalent, the "gunk" or "slime" tank, but they will get most satisfaction from the feeling which comes when a clever play on words is understood.

Many nine-year-olds have an inbuilt fear of the practical joke. This is because they are at an age where they are highly vulnerable to feeling exposed or humiliated. Their confidence and growing sense of independence are hard won, and it can be seriously threatened by experiences which embarrass them or leave them feeling diminished. They hate to be the butt of jokes and cannot easily tolerate being laughed at.

The Harry Potter books strike exactly the right note in this respect. The nine-year-old reader (or film viewer) is able to enter wholeheartedly into the world of magic tricks. The magical inventions of the Weasley twins are the Hogwarts equivalent of old-fashioned tricks such as fake blood or pretend dog pooh. The boys come up with all kinds of weird and wonderful magic with which they entertain Harry and his friends. They also use it strategically to get revenge on the bullying of Draco Malfoy and his followers. Nine-year-olds can watch the discomfort of Malfoy, safe in the knowledge that they are on the side of good against evil. Add to these delights the fact that it all happens out of sight of the parents at a boarding school and the hero is a boy who is an orphan with an exotic history and you have the perfect ingredients for latency-aged fiction.

4

Worries

Worries in the family

Even when children are protected from events in the news, they are likely to pick up on anxiety in their parents, teachers and the community at large. Parents will be familiar with the way their young children seem to know they are worried about something, even when they have been terribly careful not to talk about it in front of them.

Johnny was off his food and complained of a tummy ache. He did not want to go to school, even though it was Wednesday (his favourite day). He stayed in bed and ate nothing but eventually asked to come down and play on the computer. The next day, he again refused to go to school. His mother thought that there must be something going on, bullying perhaps, and contacted his teacher. She could shed no light on the problem. After another week, in which Johnny went to school on only two days, his mother tackled him about what was wrong, telling him firmly that she simply did not believe his story about tummy aches. Through tears, Johnny told her that he thought if he stayed at home he could make sure she was safe and that Daddy did not pack his bags to leave. He said that he had noticed the way they stopped talking whenever he and his brother came in to the room. He knew they were short of money because he had seen a pile of bills and he had overheard his father saying that there was a good job to be had in Newcastle. Johnny's mother was able to reassure him that there was no question of Daddy leaving them. They had been talking about the possibility of reorganization at Daddy's work and one option might be a move to Newcastle but they had not wanted to worry the boys.

It could be argued that Johnny's parents had no reason to let their children know that they were thinking of a move. Indeed, this may be a clear example of something which really is adult business. However, it may also be that they were more preoccupied than they had realized and that they were not always careful about when they started their whispered conversations on the subject. Johnny is clearly a very sensitive child and it may be that his suspicions link with some experience they did not know about, such as something happening to a friend's family or something seen on a television programme. Children of this age are usually ready to be reassured, so long as there is no reason to suspect that they are being fobbed off with half-truths. They would prefer, on the whole, to be free to return to their latency world of relatively uncomplicated play and learning.

Life and death

When an actual death occurs, children may try to manage their feelings by appearing to shrug it off as unimportant. Children may avoid "knowing" about the death of a close family member and may indulge in the kinds of comments and behaviour which can lead adults to think they are insensitive or uncaring. At this age, children have usually grasped the fact that death is final and do not expect animals or people to spring back into life again. They have usually recognized that not even Daddy or a favourite teacher can mend a dead creature. If they cannot deny the death by looking for the person to be mended, they may simply try to opt out of the whole event by pretending it has not happened. On the other hand, the death of a relative or even of a pet may plunge an eight-year-old child into the depths of despair, as if the world is ending. For this child, it may be that the death has brought him sharply up against knowledge of his own mortality, or possibly that of his parents. With this might come worries about what happens to a dead person, as well as worries about how he would cope if left alone in the world.

Children can also be overwhelmed by events they hear about in the news. After the terrorist attacks on New York in 2001, children became very conscious of aeroplanes flying overhead and many had nightmares about their own buildings collapsing. After the Asian tsunami of 2004 some children became anxious about being at the seaside and these fears were rekindled by pictures of New Orleans in 2005. After the shooting of an 11-year-old boy in Liverpool in 2007, hundreds of children were too frightened to go out on the streets and school attendance dipped significantly. Stories about children being abducted have a very direct impact, more direct probably than pictures of starving children in Africa. This is almost certainly because they can imagine themselves into the first situation but can distance themselves effectively from the second.

When a missing child is featured in news bulletins, a sensitive eight- or nine-year-old may become very preoccupied with the story. It is sometimes difficult for a parent to understand why a child is so upset by something which has happened to a stranger. This is because the child herself may not know what it is that she finds so compelling. It may be that the story resonates with something in her internal world, something which is not readily available to conscious thought. One such example might be the child who watches the news of a six-year-old being snatched and worries about the safety of her own six-year-old sister. This is not a simple matter of altruistic concern. She has always had ambivalent feelings about her sister. She now feels extra protective because she is unconsciously worried that her hostility might bring about a similar disaster.

Latency-aged children often suffer pangs of guilt and anxiety in relation to their unspoken thoughts and feelings. At eight and nine years of age, they are very aware of right and wrong and are inclined to feel burdened if they know they have been mean or aggressive. Just as in the example above, they often fear that their hostile thoughts will have disastrous consequences. Some children develop rituals, repeated behaviours which are designed to reassure themselves that nothing bad will happen.

> Tyrone's "habits" had become a real problem for the family. He had always been a "fussy" child but by the time he was nine, he organized his entire life according to his own unwritten rule book. He washed his hands repeatedly at home and would not dry them on anything but his own towel. He would not eat food which had touched anybody else's plate and his personal mug had to be washed separately. His bedroom was immaculately clean and tidy and he would become hysterical if anybody went in and moved anything. Bedtimes were particularly problematic as Tyrone would work his way steadily through his rituals. If anything interrupted his sequence of washing, teeth brushing, clothes folding and so on, he would have to start again. His mother had to say the same words in the same order before she turned off the light.

> If all of these routines and rituals were in place at home, Tyrone could cope in school. He was doing well with his work and he was able to be more relaxed there; less concerned about cleanliness and less fearful of contamination. His teacher knew about his difficulties but, apart from very minor concessions, she would not allow him to do things differently from the rest of the class.

Tyrone's parents sought advice as to how to understand Tyrone's bizarre behaviour. They were distressed to think that their son felt so unsafe at home and so much safer at school. The school counsellor who met with them could not be sure, but talked in a general way about the likelihood that children develop rituals as a way of convincing themselves that they can control what happens to the people they love. She suggested that Tyrone might be worried not so much that he would be harmed, but more that his "germs" would harm them. His rituals might be a way of trying to ensure their safety. This sounded strange but Tyrone's mother thought it made some sense. It gave her the courage to launch a bit of a campaign to help Tyrone break some of his habits, to show him in a very active way that she could be strong and that the family could survive whatever it was he was frightened of. She was surprised by how readily he took to this new regime and, step by step, he gave up many of his habits. The bedtime rituals could not be shifted and in the end, his parents decided to leave well alone and hope that he would be motivated to tackle this residual problem himself when he wanted to go on a sleepover or a school journey.

Secret anxieties and hidden fears

Many eight- and nine-year-olds conduct ordinary school and social lives whilst battling secretly with problems which, though hidden, take up a disproportionate amount of mental space and energy. Indeed, the effort required to keep the secret is often such that other areas of the child's development may be seriously compromised or neglected.

The following description of an event in a primary school may serve to illustrate some of the more common kinds of difficulties which children of this age do not want to acknowledge.

Mr Gomez's class were told of a plan for a three-day school journey which would involve spending a night at a residential field centre in a rural setting some 50 miles away. They had known that their year group were offered this opportunity but somehow they had never believed they would get there. They immediately felt much more grown-up. Excitement broke out in the classroom as the children turned to their friends and began to negotiate who would share rooms, who would sit next to whom on the coach and so on. A small group of boys were already outdoing each other with stories about how much spending money they would bring and another group was asking the teacher whether they could bring their video game consoles with them. The teacher, Mr Gomez, was not listening. His attention was on John, who had gone very pale, and on Susie, who was staring out of the window, looking tearful. Omar was asking to be excused. Mr Gomez made a mental note that these three children would need to be thought about individually and that he might need to speak to their parents. He knew from previous years that the field trip always brought some secret fears out into the open. He had known children who were worried that there would be nothing they could eat, others who had never been away from home and who were not sure they could manage without the reassuring bedtime rituals and the favourite cuddly toy. Another common problem was bed-wetting, with individual children feeling that they would never be able to take part in school trips because their dreadful secret might be exposed.

Many eight-year-old children need active help to manage their first sleepover, just as they needed help at three years of age to let go of their parent to attend nursery, pre-kindergarten or playgroup. For most children, the process starts with visits to other children's houses. Playing with other children's toys in somebody else's house and eating a meal with a family other than one's own are important rites of passage. Family holidays, whether spent in hotels, self-catering accommodation or on a campsite, are significant steps towards sleeping away from home without the family. Many children practise by spending time with grandparents or other members of the extended family.

By the age of eight or nine, children may well be in the midst of a social life which includes opportunities such as "play dates" or sleepovers. Most children want to take up these opportunities but it is a big step to put oneself in the hands of someone else's parents for a whole night.

Karen and Stacey were best friends at school. They lived in the same neighbourhood and spent a lot of time at each other's houses. Karen had stayed at Stacey's house a number of times. The first time had been when the girls were only six. Karen's mother had been called away to her parents' home in an emergency and she had asked Stacey's mother to look after Karen for a night or two. Since then, Karen stayed over fairly regularly; sometimes to enable her mother to go away and sometimes just because the girls were engrossed in an activity and did not want to stop until bedtime. Stacey had never stayed at Karen's house. She had been invited but persuaded her mother to make excuses for her. She would not discuss it and neither of the mothers could understand what the problem was. Matters came to a head when both girls were invited to a birthday sleepover at Paula's house. Karen was excited but Stacey said she did not want to go. Her mother decided that the issue had to be addressed and eventually persuaded Stacey to tell her what she was worried about. Stacey admitted that she was really terrified in case she woke up and got frightened that her parents had come to harm or gone away in her absence. She agreed that the fear did not make sense; she knew they were not going to go away and she did not worry about their safety during the school day or when they went out at night, leaving her with a babysitter. She said that in her own house, she knew she could slip across the landing and check on them in the night when she needed to. Her mother was amused by the reversal of roles, but managed not to laugh, and instead suggested that she talk to Karen's mum to see if they could work out a plan.

Karen's mother came up with an idea. Stacey could have a practice run by staying over at their house. She could keep a mobile phone by her bed so she could call her parents if she needed to and she promised that she would take her home at any point in the night if she got into a panic. She even offered to set this up without telling her husband, so that Stacey need not feel embarrassed. With these safeguards in place, Stacey spent a perfectly comfortable night at Karen's. They played until they were tired out and, after a brief call home at bedtime, Stacey slept as soundly as she did at home. Two weeks later, the two girls went together to Paula's birthday party. Stacey had a mobile phone in her bag but did not think she would need to use it.

Managing ordinary change and transition

As has been emphasized, latency is a period of life in which children in ordinary circumstances value routine and predictability. Anxiety levels sometimes soar with changes which are far less demanding than those faced by children going away on a school field trip, or by Karen and Stacey. Children develop all kinds of ways of managing the anxiety which accompanies ordinary changes and transitions. Some will spend hours drawing timetables, calendars and room plans, and many love to make lists. The list functions as a kind of container for their anxiety. They make a list of their friends to reassure themselves that they have plenty. They make lists of rules which they get their friends to sign up to. They make lists of sports teams, taking ownership of the very best players. They make lists of birthday presents they would like to receive, and lists of Christmas presents they have received. If they make a list of what they want to take on holiday, they feel less anxious about the unknown destination.

An eight-year-old's capacity to manage change will depend on aspects of character but also on earlier experiences of change and separation. The child who has been helped to move away from primary carer and from home in manageable steps will have built up a solid internal sense of security which will enable him or her to face later changes and transitions with more confidence. Anxiety will never be far away, however. Every transition stirs up feelings which are associated with earlier loss and separation. For some children, this is so acute as to bring about an anxious response in the face of very small changes. This can be problematic in school where there are repeated changes of activity, of teacher, of location. Some children, even nine-year-olds, need to be given warning of each upcoming change so that they can prepare themselves.

An event such as a move of house can be simultaneously exciting and terrifying to a nine-year-old, as was the case for Chloe, whose family were moving from the centre of town into a house in a small village.

Chloe was looking forward to the move. She had said goodbye to her friends at school and had made one visit to the new school where she was due to start after the summer holidays.

On the day of the move, Chloe was up early and eager to go. The removal van was outside and was being loaded up with all the furniture and packing cases. Chloe wanted to make sure that her bicycle was not forgotten and so wheeled it up the ramp to hand it over to the removal men. One of them winked at his mate and then pulled a long face, saying, "I'm sorry love, I'm not sure we can take bicycles." Chloe turned on her heel and ran back down the ramp. She did not hear the man calling after her as she pedalled off down the pavement and into the nearby park. Her father found her sitting under a tree in floods of tears. She did not want to move. She loved the old house and her school. It wasn't fair!

The removal man's ill-judged joke had unleashed a range of feelings which Chloe had not been in touch with at all. She had genuinely believed that it was all an exciting adventure – all gains, no losses. It did not take her long to regain her composure and say some fond farewells to the house they were leaving. Her father was sensitive to her upset and suggested they take the bike in the boot of the car. When they got to the new house, she was able to unload it and set off immediately to explore the village.

5

Reward and Punishment

Eight- and nine-year-old children are usually eager to please and concerned not to disappoint the adults who matter to them. Schools capitalize on this characteristic by constructing elaborate systems of reward and punishment, with the emphasis on reward where possible. Most classrooms are highly competitive places with children earning praise or rewards for good work and for good behaviour. Poor work or bad behaviour earns children the disapproval of their teacher and probably results in the loss of privileges. Most schools have a points or sticker system which allows each individual child to work their way towards a reward. The reward may be something concrete such as a sweet, a pencil or a tiny puzzle, or it may be first choice of activity in "free choice". Bad behaviour such as lack of concentration, chatting or arguing may be punished by loss of points or by an immediate sanction such as loss of playtime. Eight- and nine-year-old children grasp the rules of this kind of system quickly and the clever ones will manipulate it very easily. Others will be dispirited by never getting to the top of the sticker tree or by losing more points than they gain.

It is arguably the case that all such systems lose their potency in time. Like any currency, stickers become devalued if they are given out too readily.

Classroom reward systems

For seven- to eight-year-olds, the reward system is often one in which the whole class works together to earn a reward. There is usually very little singling out of children at this age. A creative version is one in which the teacher gives marbles to children when she has reason to praise them and the marbles accumulate in a jar. When the jar is full, the class gets a reward. For eight- to nine-year-olds, this kind of system usually gives way to one in which children are encouraged to be more competitive, both with themselves and with each other, as in the following examples.

Observations

In one class of eight- to nine-year-olds, the sticker system involved children in filling up all the spaces on a card (very like a loyalty card in a high street coffee outlet). A girl cheered as she realized she had completed her card and could therefore collect her reward from the prize bag. The teacher told her to choose something but did not notice the girl's crestfallen look when nothing further was said and nobody showed any interest in the prize she selected. In this same classroom it was interesting to see the variety of responses to being allowed to select a prize. Some children held their trophy up to gloat over their classmates whilst others took the prize almost secretly and quickly hid it in their bag or coat pocket. Each child would have a different reason for reacting the way they did. Some would be genuinely proud, others rather condescendingly triumphant. The children who hid their booty might have felt worried about being envied by others, might fear that it could be stolen, or might be uncomfortable about having got it in the first place. Did they really deserve it? Did they cheat? Did somebody else deserve it more?

In another class of eight- to nine-year-olds, the teacher jotted down names on the board. The column on the right was for children who had done something well and the column on the left for children who had done something wrong or who had behaved badly. If your name appeared twice on the left-hand side, there would be a punishment of some kind, for example loss of playtime or a chore such as tidying up at the end of the lesson. It is clear how this system resonated with the biblical idea of the sheep and the goats and also with the world of football, where a yellow card is a warning and a second yellow becomes a red card, and with it, a sending off. The teacher would stop the class from time to time and draw everyone's attention to the board, pointing out which children were on a first warning and how the general tally between the two columns was going. A positive element seemed to be the fact that the names were all rubbed off at the end of the day, so that there could be a fresh start for everyone next morning. The children seemed to respond well to this very visual, public warning system, but it was worrying that the focus was very much more on the negative list than on the positive. Nobody seemed particularly interested when a name was added to the positive side.

It is difficult to imagine a classroom running without any credit and debit system but the above examples perhaps serve to show how devalued they can become if they are not managed mindfully. Children can be acquisitive and are certainly competitive, but at eight and nine they care most about fairness and they are usually very responsive to praise and to displeasure.

Reward and punishment at home

Families have very different styles and traditions when it comes to disciplining children. Some parents find that it is enough to praise children when they behave well and express disapproval when they behave badly. Of course, individual children vary enormously in how they respond to praise and some care much more than others if they are told they have displeased their parents. Some households work on systems which are not so very different from those described in the classroom observations above, with children earning rewards and losing privileges. Parents can get into complex negotiations about time spent at the computer or in front of the television. Bedtimes are perhaps the most common flashpoints, particularly when there are a number of siblings vying for position. In some friendship groups there is a certain peer group status to be gained from reporting that one is "grounded" or cannot touch one's video game console for a week! Just as in the classroom, the reward and punishment system can become so divorced from the emotional experience (of child and parent) that it becomes a mere exercise in bargaining. Eight- and nine-year-olds certainly have a highly developed sense of justice. "It's not fair!" is a favourite rejoinder. They are usually quick to complain if they feel they are getting unfair treatment, falling back on comparisons with what their siblings or friends are allowed to do.

There is no failsafe way to discipline an unruly or disrespectful eight- or nine-year-old but parents who struggle to get in touch with the emotional experience of the child, and to find out what is driving the behaviour, are more likely to find a way to manage it. Children need boundaries and an awareness of consequences, but they also need to know that their behaviour has an impact and is thought about.

6

Relationships

Awareness of difference

By the time they reach eight or nine years of age, children are beginning to get a clear idea as to who they are and how they fit into their family and wider community. Children between eight and nine are becoming increasingly aware of the differences between themselves and others. They begin to form clear views as to who is cleverer than whom, who is the best at drawing, maths, sport, writing and so on. They also consolidate their ideas as to where they themselves fit in. Most have to come to terms with not being "the best" at anything but hopefully they will find comfort in knowing what their relative strengths are. For a small minority, comparing themselves with others is a very painful process. Recognizing that one is not particularly good at anything is painful enough but if the child also has unrewarding relationships at home and cannot make friends at school, the situation can feel intolerable. These are the children who may resort to ways of ridding themselves of these unwelcome feelings. The kinds of behaviours which may result include attacks of an overt or covert kind on themselves or on other children.

> Billy was a small, pale eight-year-old boy with fair, spiky hair and thick-lensed spectacles. He was a slow learner who had made some progress with reading since coming into the year group but his writing was of a very poor standard. He had difficulty holding his pencil steady and he could not make his letters sit on the lines. His teacher was keen to encourage him and offered praise whenever she could. She was puzzled as to why this did not seem to please him. He would look away and shuffle his feet under the desk, covering his work with his hands. When he did a reasonable piece of work on "Whales" she took

the opportunity to hold his book up for the class to see, inviting them to applaud him for earning a gold sticker. Billy went very red in the face and, although he took the sticker, he did not put it on his jumper. She was horrified when, later the same day, she found Billy's work in the bin, torn in two. She had not understood that a child with such low self-esteem sometimes finds praise intolerable. If it does not resonate with an internal feeling of pride in the work, the child can feel further humiliated. Billy could not express his feelings to his teacher, so turned his anger and frustration into an attack on the work.

Jason's behaviour was very different. On the surface, he did not seem to care what his work looked like. When his teacher tried to help him, he would hop from foot to foot, insisting that he understood, "Yeah, yeah, OK". He appeared not to notice the difference in quality between his own work and that of his immediate friendship group. He had difficulty with reading and writing but was quick witted and kept the class entertained with his clowning around, particularly when they were being supervised by a classroom helper or supply teacher. The other children enjoyed this aspect of his behaviour but were also deeply irritated by another of his habits. He found it very difficult to focus on his own work and was forever leaning over the table, reaching out with his pencil to draw a quick squiggle on his neighbour's page. He sometimes found an excuse to cross the classroom, pausing at each table to laugh at somebody's work or crumple it quickly, saying "Whoops, sorry!" The owner of the damaged work would call out to the teacher, who would issue a threat to Jason and encourage the victim to rub out the squiggle or start again. It all seemed very unfair but the teacher was at a loss to know how to control this volatile, charming rogue.

In similar circumstances, Miriam's behaviour was different again. She lapped up praise from her teacher and if none was on offer, would take her book around the classroom demanding that her peers admire her work. At the end of every lesson, she asked if she could have a sticker and if the teacher refused her, she would go to the classroom assistant and ask again. A few weeks before the Christmas holidays, a strange and troubling thing began to happen. Exercise books were disappearing from children's trays. At first the teacher put it down to carelessness and suggested that everyone take time to tidy up the classroom. However, it soon became clear that somebody was stealing the books.

The teacher talked to the class and when the situation did not improve, asked for the headteacher to become involved. A letter went home to all the parents. A few days later, Miriam's mother came in to see the headteacher. She was very upset and angry. She told the head that she had thought there was something odd in the way her daughter was behaving and so had gone to look in her room and, under the bed, had found a small pile of exercise books. Miriam had eventually admitted that she had taken them because she was envious of the clever children.

Special needs

The term *special needs* covers a vast range of developmental, cognitive, behavioural and emotional difficulties. Some are genetic, some organic and some environmental. In an average classroom there may be many different versions of *special needs* in evidence. There are likely to be one or two children with a diagnosis of ADHD (attention deficit hyperactivity disorder) and possibly one or two with Asperger syndrome or autistic spectrum disorder. If it is a designated school, there may also be children with disabilities such as cerebral palsy, muscular dystrophy or Down's syndrome.

As with all kinds of "difference", familiarity is helpful in reducing fear and prejudice. The way individual children manage themselves in relation to the child with special needs will depend on previous experience and parental attitudes, as well as on much less tangible features of their own internal world. Some children love to look after their wheelchair-bound classmate. It is as if they lodge all their own vulnerability and neediness in a child with disabilities and then take care of it by looking after the dependent child. Much will, of course, also depend on the internal world of the child with a special need. Some are consumed with feelings of envy and resentment which get in the way of forming ordinary friendly relationships with their able-bodied peers. Others seem to be "little angels", never complaining and always having to suppress their envy and hostility.

In *Understanding Your Young Child with Special Needs* Pamela Bartram (2007) explores these issues in detail and gives examples of ways in which "an emotionally lively connection" may be achieved.

A small number of children may be unable to cope with disability and may behave in ways which seem at best insensitive and, at worst, cruel. These may be individuals who simply cannot face the reality of pain and distress and whose only concern is to distance themselves from it or to attack it. This is unusual, but can occur between peers. It can also occur where there is a parent with a disability as in the following example.

Steven's father was diagnosed with multiple sclerosis when he was just six years old. At first, it was hardly noticeable and Steven was simply told that there would be times when his dad was not feeling well and could not do some of the things they used to like doing together, such as flying kites in the park. Three years later, Steven's father's condition had worsened and he was very depressed. Steven's mother was exhausted and worried about the family finances but she was determined to look on the bright side. She expected Steven to be loving towards his father and not complain about the restrictions the disease had placed on their lives. Steven felt full of rage and he could barely contain himself when his father asked him to go upstairs to fetch his slippers. He longed to shout at him to get up and fetch them himself. He despised what he saw as his father's self-pity. Why had he got lumbered with an invalid for a father? He found himself imagining what it would feel like to kick his father's sticks away. This recurrent thought made him feel so full of guilt and self-loathing that he would have difficulty sleeping at night.

Fortunately Steven's grandmother was able to intervene. She could see that Steven was carrying all the anger which her daughter and son-in-law were not able to acknowledge. She could recognize how Steven was suffering from the loss of a vibrant male role model and how much he feared falling victim to the disease himself. Her daughter did not want her to voice these thoughts but she persevered, and it helped Steven to feel that somebody understood something of his experience. He was then able to feel less critical of his father and, over time, to find ways in which they could still enjoy each other's company.

Particular talents

Some parents devote considerable amounts of time, energy and money to maximizing their children's opportunities in a particular direction. Where a specific talent or aptitude has been identified, it is common to find parents putting aspects of their own lives on hold to ensure that their child is given every assistance to achieve his or her goal. Whether the child's potential is in swimming, dancing, ice skating, go-karting or playing a musical instrument, the sacrifices are much the same.

This single-minded pursuit of success may be necessary in some fields, but it can distort ordinary family life and there is a huge risk involved. If the child becomes a concert pianist, represents the country in the Olympics or plays in a national team sport, it will all feel worthwhile. However, there have always been some parents who push their relatively untalented children forward. Some stage or dance schools, for example, seem to be run more for the ambitions of the parents than for the enjoyment of the children. The current public preoccupation with fame and celebrity is leading many families to invest hope in unattainable goals. It is also leading many children to prize fame above everything. It is a difficult task, but parents who manage to balance pursuit of success in a particular field with sufficient ordinary family life experience are probably those who best help their children to stay in touch with reality and learn to manage the pain of failure as well as the thrill of success.

Gender

Boys and girls tend to be intolerant of each other in this stage of development. Boys think girls are feeble or stupid and girls think boys are insensitive or rough. A group of children were photographed for the classroom wall and each was asked to give a brief description of themselves, naming their friends and identifying their likes and dislikes. It was striking that all the girls listed other girls as their friends and chose interests such as pets and collecting Barbie® doll accessories. The boys named other boys as their friends and identified their hobbies as sports and watching their favourite soccer team. There are, of course, exceptions to this rule. Some boys and girls give each other a wide berth when they are in full view of their single-sex friendship groups at school, but come together in their neighbourhood in the evening and at weekends. Boy and girl cousins may "blank" each other at school but play happily when their families get together in the holidays. There are also the boys and girls who do not stick to type but who attach themselves resolutely to groups of the opposite gender. The obvious example is the girl who longs to be accepted by the soccer-playing boys. If she has sufficient skills, she may well be included in their games, but she will probably be disowned by the other girls in the process. Similarly, there are boys who prefer the quieter company of girls and every class of eight- and nine-year-olds will probably have at least one boy–girl pair who seem inseparable.

Race, religion and ethnicity

Children of eight and nine have usually become aware of differences of race, culture, language and religion. Their understanding of the complexity of the differences between people will not be well developed and splits may occur along very crude lines. Hassan was a boy who talked about his Somali customs and beliefs in a provocative way. His peers did not understand that he did so as a way of making himself feel better when he was being ostracized by the group. They simply thought he was showing off and that led them to retaliate by accusing him of being a "terrorist" and laughing at the girls in the class who were wearing the hijab. The other Muslim boys then felt they had to intervene to defend the girls. Teachers have a responsibility to prevent this kind of undigested political propaganda from being reproduced in the classroom, and fortunately for Hassan, he had a teacher who was prepared to tackle the issues.

Hassan was attending an inner city school in which there were children from all over the world, with over 40 different languages represented. A great deal of progress has been made in schools such as this one, where the ethos is an inclusive one and where the curriculum takes full account of the multiethnic nature of the groups. Where schools educate the children in the main principles of all religions and take care to remember all the different festivals, there is likely to be much less prejudice and suspicion. It is, however, another area in which children may find themselves with split loyalties. Do they embrace the values being taught at school or remain in line with their parents' position, which may be one of ignorance and intolerance?

For many families with strict religious rules or cultural norms, there are conflicts which may be hard to resolve. The following is an example from the experience of a Sikh family, where the mother did not speak any English and the father was away for much of the year.

> Harjinder's mother had always been rather proud of her eight-year-old son's good manners. She had taught him to respect his elders and he had always been a credit to her when the extended family visited. She was very shocked and distressed when he started to be rude and challenging halfway through the first term of the new school year. He would get home from school and start complaining immediately. He did not want the food she had prepared, he wanted to watch what she considered to be unsuitable television programmes and he would not

settle to do his homework. When she tried to tell him off, he retaliated by talking to her in English. When she got angry, he put his hands over his ears, which she found very provocative. Most evenings, she would send him to bed early and he would shrug. What did he care?

This went on for some weeks, with Harjinder's behaviour escalating and his mother becoming more and more despairing and ashamed. She repeatedly told him to wait until his father got back from India. Harjinder's mother wondered if she should go to the school and ask about her son's behaviour, but she had never felt comfortable there and without Harjinder to translate, she did not know how she would cope. A week or two later, she received a letter from the headteacher and with it an invitation to meet with the home–school liaison worker. She went to the meeting and was able to communicate with Harjinder's teacher, through the Punjabi-speaking interpreter. It emerged that the teacher was also worried about Harjinder. His work was deteriorating and he looked very unhappy in class. She had noticed that he no longer joined in with his classmates at break times but gravitated towards the Sikh boys in the year group above. She suggested that the liaison worker arrange to make a home visit.

At the home visit, Harjinder was able to speak about the fact that he did not know what to do. He was an outsider in his class and wanted to be loyal to his race and culture, but some of the older boys were anti-English and that frightened him.

Harjinder was doing what many children do when they find themselves in such deeply felt conflict. At school he was separating himself from the dominant peer culture by identifying with the older Sikh boys. He wanted his father to be proud of him when he returned. At home, he was punishing his mother by behaving like the uncouth "westernized" boy she feared he could become. Neither version was real. The truth was that Harjinder had grown up in London and he had two languages and two cultures. He had adopted some aspects of the local culture but he did not want to reject his heritage. He simply needed help with recognizing the pressures and finding a way through which would suit him and his family.

Bullying

Wherever there is perceived difference, there is scope for bullying to surface. There are very few children who would deny that they have taken part in some form of bullying at some stage in their primary school careers. Most will also admit to having been bullied. Bullying arises from a simple psychological manoeuvre, usually unconscious, which, if acted upon, can have a devastating impact on the victim. The manoeuvre goes as follows: "I don't want to feel small, poor or stupid so I will make somebody else feel those things." The target may be anybody who is smaller, weaker, less accomplished or simply "different". They may not actually be any of those things, but if they are ready to believe it, they will slip into the role of victim all too quickly and easily.

Of course, bullying takes many forms and some of it is very serious indeed. Schools need to have policies with clear strategies and consequences which everyone understands. If left unchallenged, bullies can become addicted to the experience and the stakes will become higher and higher as the bullying becomes more extreme. The bullies then have to surround themselves with more and more "supporters" who act as protection against any potential retaliation. There are particular dangers in internet bullying. Bullies who use the internet are able to distance themselves from what they are doing; they can imagine but do not have to witness the distress of their victims. Children who have joined in with bullying on social networking websites such as MySpace have said that they did not really think of themselves as bullies; it felt so impersonal.

Bullying is best controlled by early intervention. However, vigilance is only part of the answer. It is also important to give children opportunities to talk about their experiences, both as bullies and as victims of bullying. Classroom initiatives such as circle time, and SEAL (social and emotional aspects of learning) in England and Wales, and their equivalents in other countries, can provide opportunities for eight- and nine-year-olds to reflect on the meaning of bullying behaviour and to learn from each other experience as well as their own.

Language and sexuality

In many playgrounds in the early years of the twenty-first century, language is much less restrained and parents have a difficult corrective job to do if they want their children not to swear or use too much slang. Television is very influential in moulding children's expressive language. An eight-year-old girl stunned her parents into silence when her response to being asked to brush her hair was to turn on them, shrug her shoulders and say in a slow drawl, "Whatever". Many latency-aged children use gestures which they have seen in the playground or the street but which they do not fully understand. They may need help to know that teachers do not like to be shrugged at, that they must never hold up two fingers and they should not tell their grandmother that their supply teacher is "crap".

> Christopher had got very excited at playtime and he had gone up to a group of girls in his class, saying boldly that he would like to "sex them up". They giggled at first and this served only to encourage him. He danced around them shouting, "Sex you up. Sex you up. Sex you up and you like it." The girls began to feel uneasy and they told him to go away. He was enjoying himself and he continued to circle around them. Sylvia suddenly burst into tears and her friends huddled round her. One girl told Christopher to "buzz off" and he became even more excited: "You swore, you swore, you did." By this time the playground supervisor had heard the commotion and was approaching. She grabbed Christopher by the arm and marched him off indoors, telling the girls to follow.
>
> Christopher's mother was horrified to receive a call from the school. She could not understand what Christopher had been thinking of. She was very angry and took him home in silence. It was not until bedtime that she tried to talk to him. By now he was silent and tearful and she got nowhere. When his father tried a little later, Christopher asked him, "What does 'sex you up' mean?" He had only a vague idea and had repeated it because he had heard some older boys chanting it at some girls in the street. He thought the girls in his own class would be impressed.

Eight- and nine-year-olds are particularly vulnerable to getting themselves into deep water through using language in a grandiose way. This is another area in which there is scope for serious misunderstanding between home and school. Just as children play one parent off against another, or a parent off against a grandparent, they are adept at playing the teacher off against their mother or father. This may take the form of insisting that the teacher taught them a particular word or that he or she does not mind if they use it in class. Equally common is the child who insists that they are allowed to swear at home or to use sexually explicit language. Of course, if they do come from a home where swearing is the norm, they have a difficult task at school where they have to fit in with an expectation that they will control their language, even when angry or excited.

7

The Eight- and Nine-Year-Old as Consumer

Merchandise

The commercialization of childhood has proceeded at a tremendous pace since the late 1990s. The market is now flooded with clothes, toys, books and all kinds of collectables which are targeted at specific age groups. By the age of eight, children in the western cultures are usually fully fledged consumers. They know what is available, thanks to television advertising and the enticing displays of merchandise which they encounter on their way into and out of shops. Even when parents manage to restrict access to these, children see what their friends have got. Every new film or popular children's book is accompanied by "must have" memorabilia. Much of it takes the form of plastic replicas of the main characters but there will also be the dressing-up outfits, scarves, bags, pencil cases and so on. Hugely inflated prices are charged for a very ordinary item such as a ruler, simply because the logo appears at one end. The same kind of merchandise is available to tempt the supporter of a particular sports club or the fan of a top boy or girl band. Packaging of some foods is also aimed at the young child, endorsed as it appears to be by some famous sports person or pop star.

Making collections remains a central feature of the middle years of latency. Children love to collect things and to use their collections as a kind of social currency. They can boast about their acquisitions, offer to make swaps, drive hard bargains, be generous to less fortunate peers and so on. However, if the pressure is great and the items being collected are expensive, there will be the danger of provoking extortion or theft. Schools do their best to encourage children to collect things which do not cost money but are hard pressed to do so in the face of such effective marketing strategies. Many schools have rules about what can be brought into school, with electronic games, mobile phones and digital audio players being on the list of forbidden items.

It has always been difficult for the child whose parents insist on dressing them in a different way from their friends. It is all the more so now, when the obsession of "label" or "brand" has permeated right down to this age group. Even at eight, it now matters desperately that the child's trainers have a recognizable logo. Most worrying perhaps is the way in which clothing for girls of this age is designed to accentuate their femininity, or rather, their "girly-ness". The proliferation of pre-teen fashion for girls, with thongs, bikini tops, miniskirts and so on, has arguably sexualized the age group in a way which is most alarming and which presents parents and schools with a very particular challenge.

Digital technology

It takes a very determined parent to stand aside entirely from these pressures. It used to be the case that the small number of children who did not have a television at home were at a disadvantage with their peer group when it came to knowing what was going on in various programmes. There is now an expectation, among children at least, that they will have a television set in their bedrooms. They are led to believe that everyone else has one. They are also led to believe that they are the only ones not to have a video game console, a DVD player, a portable media player and a personal computer. At the turn of the millennium, it really did seem that this was becoming the norm. There has since been a backlash and parents are being encouraged to restrict their children's television viewing, to remove the television sets from the bedrooms, to limit the time spent on video games and so on. It remains to be seen how effective this campaign will be and whether it will hold back the tide of what seems like the ever-increasing power of market forces.

It is worth noting that used carefully, these electronic, digital innovations can be tremendously important in children's lives. It may be particularly so for children in the middle latency period when they need to be able to retreat from the hurly-burly of relationships and spend some time mastering new skills and acquiring new knowledge. A computer program or video game can provide children with a learning environment they can manage and a set of targets they can reach, at their own pace and in their own time.

Word processing programs can boost the confidence of the child who finds it difficult to write and many of the art programs can promote creativity, as in the following example.

> Nine-year-old Sue and her ten-year-old neighbour, Tara, were at Sue's house one day in the school holidays. Sue's mother was at her computer and asked the children to leave her in peace to get on with her work. They were forbidden to watch television and they felt bored and resentful. Mrs Gregg suggested they do some drawing, or go out in the garden, or read a book. They replied grumpily that they didn't have any ideas.
>
> The two children astonished Mrs Gregg by staying out of her way for nearly two hours. She emerged from her study feeling rather guilty about leaving them so long. They were desperate to show her what they had been up to. They had decided to do some drawing and this had developed into making models with paper and card and pipe cleaners. Sue had made a witch and this had led them to think about Red Riding-Hood. They had quickly made a full set of characters and wondered about a puppet theatre. Then the brainwave had struck. They would take the figures out into the garden and take photos, making the long grass look like the forest and so on. The bird bath

could be a lake and they could make the grandmother's house out of sticks. They had used Sue's mother's camera and were now eager to put the whole lot together on the computer to make a slide show. They had already agreed on captions.

So many elements of latency life seemed to have come together in this enterprise. The two girls were edging towards taking up the "I'm bored" position of early adolescence when they found themselves caught up in a shared activity which rekindled many of their latency preoccupations. Drawing, cutting and sticking are the "safe" activities of the younger latency child and the story they chose was one they had actually long outgrown but had in it the familiar elements of adventure, adversity and good triumphing over evil.

The second part of their project showed a capacity to extend themselves beyond this familiar territory and make use of technology in a creative but still playful way.

Diet and exercise

A great deal of attention is currently being paid to the question of diet and childhood obesity. There is research evidence to show that children are eating more fatty foods, more salt and more sugar. They are also taking less exercise. The role of advertising and the media is being called into question, with controls being imposed on the promotion of junk food. Many schools in the UK have jettisoned tuck shops and vending machines and most primary schools have banned sugary snacks, replacing them with a mid-morning piece of fruit. Some local authorities have instituted "walk to school days" and have organized groups of parents to escort groups of children. Apart from the obvious fact that human beings feel stronger and healthier when they eat sensibly and take regular exercise, there is also a clear link between healthy eating and the capacity to concentrate and to learn.

Unfortunately the campaign to promote healthy school meals has not been immediately successful in all areas of the UK. Many families resent what they see as heavy-handed interference, whilst others simply do not want to believe the evidence. It is hard for parents to "deprive" their children of what they themselves prefer to eat, particularly in communities where there have been entrenched patterns of poverty and deprivation. It is also hard for children to "educate" their parents in this respect, although it remains to be seen whether, in the long term, their experience at school will influence their attitudes to diet and exercise.

On an individual level, eating remains a source of great enjoyment for some, whilst for others it is an area of conflict and high anxiety. By the time children are eight or nine years of age, they usually have well-established likes and dislikes and mealtimes provide the backdrop for many a family drama. Providing nourishment is one of the basic tasks of parenthood and children of all ages have a way of tuning into their parents' particular anxieties. As the mother of one "faddy" nine-year-old said, "He knows which buttons to press." She added that it had been the same when he was a baby; he seemed to know when she was tired and over-stretched and would take an age over his feed. Children who reject food are usually more worrying to parents than children who overeat and there is often a need for a third person, whether family member or professional, to intervene in order to stop anxiety from escalating in both parent and child. This is the age at which children's love of animals may lead them to become vegetarian or they may suddenly demand organic food or food with a small carbon footprint. Some of these enthusiasms are short-lived; others become part of the individual's developing identity.

Minor eating difficulties are usually accessible to behavioural strategies but some are indicative of more serious underlying problems related to worries about body image, about growing up, separating, competing at school and so on. A dramatic change in the eating habits of a nine-year-old probably does need to be taken seriously. Being able to eat a variety of foods in a variety of settings is an important factor in being able to develop a social life outside the home and family.

8

Summary

Moving on

There is something deeply significant about reaching double figures. In some educational systems, children who are 10 or 11 years old will soon move from primary to secondary school.

Children who are "nearly ten" have come a long way since they were "just eight" and most will be looking ahead eagerly to the next stage. However, in any group of children reaching their tenth birthday, there will be some who are physically, psychologically and emotionally ready to move on and others who are reluctant to leave the relatively calm waters of latency.

As a generalization, children approaching their tenth birthday have a coherent picture of who they are and how they fit into the bigger picture of home, family and school. They have developed some understanding of their own strengths and weaknesses and clear ideas about what they like and dislike and what they do and do not care about. Most "nearly tens" are able to recognize that they have a personal history and will be interested to hear about it from their parents and grandparents. They will also be able to think into the future with some notion as to what they might hope to achieve. Their ambitions may be somewhat unrealistic but they are at least able to imagine themselves as having a role in the adult world. They no longer see things in simple terms, as either right or wrong, but begin to be able to encompass a range of views and even to acknowledge their own ambivalent feelings. Children at the end of the eight–nine-year period are often experimenting with new friendships and are beginning to focus on what it means to belong to different kinds of small groups. Children who are nine-and-three-quarter years old are ready to disagree with some of what their parents hold dear and they may suddenly seem less amenable and more argumentative. For the past two or three years, their energies have been directed towards the acquisition of knowledge and skills; now they turn back to focus more fully on the world of human relationships.

References

Bartram, P. (2007) *Understanding Your Young Child with Special Needs.* London: Jessica Kingsley Publishers.

Emanuel, L. (2005) *Understanding Your Three-Year-Old.* London: Jessica Kingsley Publishers.

ChildLine (1999) *Suddenly...99 Short Stories for the Millennium.* High Wycombe: Staples.

Youell, B. (2006) *The Learning Relationship: Psychoanalytic Thinking in Education.* London: Karnac.

Helpful Organizations

Bullying UK
185 Tower Bridge Road
London SE1 2UF
Tel: 020 7378 1446
www.bullying.co.uk
Advice for victims of bullying and their parents

ChildLine
45 Folgate Street
London E1 6GL
Tel: 020 7650 3200
Helpline: 0800 111 (for children and young people)
www.childline.org.uk
Confidential 24-hour helpline for children and young people

Exploring Parenthood
Latimer Education Centre
194 Freston Road
London W10 6TT
Tel: 020 8964 1827
Parents' Advice Line: 020 8960 1678
Advice on parenting problems from newborn to adult

Gingerbread Association for One Parent Families
7 Sovereign Close
London E1W 2HW
Tel: 020 7488 9300
Advice Line: 0800 018 4318 (Monday to Friday 9 a.m. to 5 p.m.)
www.gingerbread.org.uk
Support for single-parent families

Parentline Plus (formerly National Stepfamily Association)
Tel: 0808 800 2222 (helpline 24 hours a day)
www.parentlineplus.org.uk
Information and support for parents and stepparents

YoungMinds/National Association for Child and Family Mental Health
102–108 Clerkenwell Road
London EC1M 5SA
Tel: 020 7336 8445
Parents' Information Service: 0800 018 2138
www.youngminds.org.uk
Campaign to improve the mental health of children and young people

Index

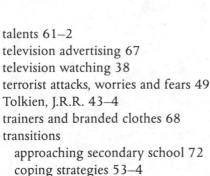